50 British Pub Recipes for Home

By: Kelly Johnson

Table of Contents

- Fish and Chips
- Shepherd's Pie
- Beef Wellington
- Steak and Ale Pie
- Bangers and Mash
- Ploughman's Lunch
- Toad in the Hole
- Bubble and Squeak
- Full English Breakfast
- Chicken Tikka Masala
- Scotch Eggs
- Cornish Pasty
- Lancashire Hotpot
- Welsh Rarebit
- Steak and Kidney Pie
- Chicken and Leek Pie
- Pork Pie
- Black Pudding
- Sunday Roast (with Yorkshire Pudding)
- Cottage Pie
- Spotted Dick
- Sticky Toffee Pudding
- Trifle
- Eton Mess
- Crumpets
- Scones with Clotted Cream and Jam
- Fish Pie
- Cock-a-Leekie Soup
- Beef Stew and Dumplings
- Mince and Tatties
- Chicken and Mushroom Pie
- Apple Crumble
- Bread and Butter Pudding
- Cheese and Onion Pie
- Corned Beef Hash

- Chicken Balti
- Gammon Steak with Pineapple
- Lamb Shank
- Prawn Cocktail
- Beef Bourguignon
- Rabbit Stew
- Liver and Onions
- Chicken Liver Pâté
- Mushy Peas
- Pea and Ham Soup
- Leek and Potato Soup
- Stilton and Broccoli Soup
- Salmon en Croute
- Haggis, Neeps, and Tatties
- Beef and Guinness Stew

Fish and Chips

Ingredients:

For the fish:

- 4 fillets of white fish (such as cod, haddock, or pollock)
- 1 cup all-purpose flour
- 1 teaspoon baking powder
- 1 teaspoon salt
- 1/2 teaspoon black pepper
- 1 cup cold beer (a light lager works well)
- Vegetable oil, for frying

For the chips:

- 4 large potatoes, peeled and cut into thick strips
- Vegetable oil, for frying
- Salt, to taste

For serving:

- Tartar sauce
- Lemon wedges
- Optional: mushy peas

Instructions:

1. Prepare the Fish:
    - In a large bowl, mix together the flour, baking powder, salt, and pepper.
    - Gradually whisk in the cold beer until you have a smooth batter.
    - Let the batter rest for about 15-20 minutes while you prepare the chips.
2. Prepare the Chips:
    - Rinse the potato strips under cold water to remove excess starch.

- Pat them dry with paper towels.
- Heat vegetable oil in a deep fryer or large pot to 325°F (165°C).
- Fry the potato strips in batches until they are just starting to soften but not yet golden, about 5-7 minutes.
- Remove the partially cooked chips from the oil and let them drain on a paper towel-lined plate.

3. Fry the Fish and Finish the Chips:
   - Increase the oil temperature to 375°F (190°C).
   - Dip each fish fillet into the batter, allowing any excess batter to drip off.
   - Carefully place the battered fish into the hot oil and fry until golden brown and crispy, about 5-7 minutes depending on the thickness of the fillets.
   - Remove the fried fish from the oil and place them on a paper towel-lined plate to drain.
4. Finish the Chips:
   - Return the partially cooked chips to the hot oil in batches and fry until golden brown and crispy, about 3-5 minutes.
   - Remove the chips from the oil and drain them on paper towels.
   - Sprinkle the hot chips with salt while they're still hot.
5. Serve:
   - Serve the hot fish and chips with tartar sauce, lemon wedges, and optional mushy peas on the side.
   - Enjoy your homemade Fish and Chips!

This recipe captures the classic flavors and textures of traditional British Fish and Chips, perfect for a delicious meal any day of the week.

Shepherd's Pie

Ingredients:

For the filling:

- 1 tablespoon olive oil
- 1 onion, diced
- 2 carrots, diced
- 2 cloves garlic, minced
- 1 pound (450g) ground lamb or beef
- 2 tablespoons all-purpose flour
- 1 cup beef or vegetable broth
- 2 tablespoons tomato paste
- 1 teaspoon Worcestershire sauce
- 1 teaspoon dried thyme
- Salt and pepper, to taste
- 1 cup frozen peas

For the mashed potato topping:

- 2 pounds (900g) potatoes, peeled and cut into chunks
- 4 tablespoons butter
- 1/2 cup milk or cream
- Salt and pepper, to taste
- 1/2 cup shredded cheddar cheese (optional)

Instructions:

1. Prepare the Filling:
    - Heat the olive oil in a large skillet over medium heat.
    - Add the diced onion and carrots and cook until softened, about 5 minutes.
    - Add the minced garlic and cook for an additional minute.
    - Add the ground lamb or beef to the skillet, breaking it up with a spoon, and cook until browned.
    - Sprinkle the flour over the meat and vegetables and stir to combine.

- Pour in the beef or vegetable broth and stir in the tomato paste, Worcestershire sauce, dried thyme, salt, and pepper.
- Simmer the filling for about 10 minutes, until thickened.
- Stir in the frozen peas and cook for an additional 2-3 minutes. Remove from heat.

2. Prepare the Mashed Potato Topping:
    - While the filling is simmering, place the peeled and chopped potatoes in a large pot of salted water.
    - Bring the water to a boil and cook the potatoes until tender, about 15-20 minutes.
    - Drain the cooked potatoes and return them to the pot.
    - Add the butter and milk or cream to the potatoes and mash until smooth.
    - Season with salt and pepper to taste.

3. Assemble and Bake:
    - Preheat your oven to 400°F (200°C).
    - Transfer the prepared filling to a baking dish and spread it out evenly.
    - Spoon the mashed potatoes over the filling, spreading them out with a spatula.
    - If desired, sprinkle shredded cheddar cheese over the mashed potatoes.
    - Place the baking dish in the preheated oven and bake for 20-25 minutes, or until the mashed potatoes are lightly golden and the filling is bubbly.
    - Remove the Shepherd's Pie from the oven and let it cool for a few minutes before serving.
    - Enjoy your hearty and comforting Shepherd's Pie!

Beef Wellington

Ingredients:

- 1 whole beef tenderloin (about 2 pounds/900g), trimmed
- Salt and freshly ground black pepper
- 2 tablespoons olive oil
- 2 tablespoons Dijon mustard
- 1 pound (450g) mushrooms, finely chopped
- 2 shallots, finely chopped
- 2 cloves garlic, minced
- 2 tablespoons butter
- 1/4 cup dry white wine or beef broth
- 1 package (17.3 ounces/490g) frozen puff pastry, thawed
- Flour, for rolling out pastry
- 1 egg, beaten (for egg wash)

Instructions:

1. Prepare the Beef:
    - Season the beef tenderloin generously with salt and pepper.
    - Heat the olive oil in a large skillet over high heat.
    - Sear the beef tenderloin on all sides until nicely browned, about 2 minutes per side. Remove from heat and let it cool.
    - Once cooled, brush the entire surface of the beef tenderloin with Dijon mustard. Set aside.
2. Prepare the Mushroom Duxelles:
    - In the same skillet used for searing the beef, melt the butter over medium heat.
    - Add the finely chopped mushrooms, shallots, and garlic to the skillet. Cook, stirring frequently, until the mushrooms release their moisture and the mixture becomes dry, about 10-12 minutes.
    - Season the mushroom mixture with salt and pepper to taste.
    - Deglaze the skillet with white wine or beef broth, scraping up any browned bits from the bottom of the pan. Cook until the liquid evaporates. Remove from heat and let the mushroom mixture cool slightly.
3. Assemble the Beef Wellington:

- On a lightly floured surface, roll out the thawed puff pastry to a rectangle large enough to wrap around the beef tenderloin.
- Spread the mushroom duxelles evenly over the puff pastry.
- Place the seared beef tenderloin on top of the mushroom duxelles.
- Carefully fold the puff pastry over the beef, sealing the edges and trimming off any excess pastry.
- Brush the top and sides of the pastry-wrapped beef with beaten egg for a golden finish.

4. Bake the Beef Wellington:
   - Preheat your oven to 425°F (220°C).
   - Place the Beef Wellington on a baking sheet lined with parchment paper.
   - Bake in the preheated oven for 35-40 minutes, or until the pastry is golden brown and the internal temperature of the beef reaches your desired level of doneness (medium-rare is around 130°F/55°C).
   - Remove the Beef Wellington from the oven and let it rest for 10 minutes before slicing.
   - Slice and serve the Beef Wellington with your favorite sides, such as mashed potatoes and roasted vegetables.
   - Enjoy this elegant and delicious dish!

Steak and Ale Pie

Ingredients:

For the filling:

- 1.5 pounds (680g) beef stew meat, cut into bite-sized pieces
- Salt and pepper, to taste
- 2 tablespoons all-purpose flour
- 2 tablespoons vegetable oil
- 1 onion, chopped
- 2 cloves garlic, minced
- 2 carrots, diced
- 2 celery stalks, diced
- 1 tablespoon tomato paste
- 1 tablespoon Worcestershire sauce
- 1 teaspoon dried thyme
- 1 teaspoon dried rosemary
- 1 cup (240ml) ale or stout beer
- 1 cup (240ml) beef broth
- 1 bay leaf
- 1 sheet of puff pastry, thawed if frozen
- 1 egg, beaten (for egg wash)

Instructions:

1. Prepare the Beef Filling:
    - Season the beef stew meat generously with salt and pepper, then toss with flour to coat.
    - Heat the vegetable oil in a large skillet or Dutch oven over medium-high heat.
    - Add the beef pieces in batches and brown them on all sides. Remove the browned beef from the skillet and set aside.
2. Cook the Vegetables:
    - In the same skillet or Dutch oven, add the chopped onion, minced garlic, diced carrots, and diced celery. Cook until the vegetables are softened, about 5-7 minutes.

3. Combine Ingredients:
   - Return the browned beef to the skillet with the vegetables.
   - Stir in the tomato paste, Worcestershire sauce, dried thyme, and dried rosemary, coating the meat and vegetables evenly.
   - Pour in the ale or stout beer and beef broth. Add the bay leaf.
   - Bring the mixture to a simmer, then reduce the heat to low. Cover and cook for 1.5 to 2 hours, or until the beef is tender and the flavors have melded together. Stir occasionally.
4. Prepare the Pastry:
   - Preheat your oven to 400°F (200°C).
   - Roll out the puff pastry on a lightly floured surface to fit the size of your baking dish. It should be slightly larger than the diameter of your dish.
5. Assemble the Pie:
   - Once the beef filling is ready, discard the bay leaf.
   - Transfer the filling to a deep pie dish or casserole dish.
   - Place the rolled-out puff pastry on top of the filling, trimming any excess pastry and crimping the edges to seal.
   - Cut a few slits in the pastry to allow steam to escape during baking.
   - Brush the top of the pastry with beaten egg for a golden finish.
6. Bake the Pie:
   - Place the assembled pie on a baking sheet to catch any drips.
   - Bake in the preheated oven for 25-30 minutes, or until the pastry is puffed and golden brown.
7. Serve:
   - Remove the Steak and Ale Pie from the oven and let it cool slightly before serving.
   - Serve slices of the pie with your favorite sides, such as mashed potatoes and steamed vegetables.
   - Enjoy this comforting and flavorful British classic!

Bangers and Mash

Ingredients:

For the sausages:

- 6-8 pork sausages (traditional British bangers)
- 1 tablespoon vegetable oil

For the mashed potatoes:

- 2 pounds (about 900g) potatoes, peeled and cut into chunks
- Salt, to taste
- 4 tablespoons butter
- 1/2 cup milk or cream
- Salt and pepper, to taste

For the onion gravy:

- 2 onions, thinly sliced
- 2 tablespoons butter
- 2 tablespoons all-purpose flour
- 2 cups beef or chicken broth
- Salt and pepper, to taste

Instructions:

1. Prepare the Sausages:
    - Heat the vegetable oil in a large skillet over medium heat.
    - Add the sausages to the skillet and cook, turning occasionally, until they are browned on all sides and cooked through, about 12-15 minutes. Remove from heat and set aside.
2. Make the Mashed Potatoes:
    - Place the peeled and chopped potatoes in a large pot of salted water.

- Bring the water to a boil and cook the potatoes until tender, about 15-20 minutes.
- Drain the cooked potatoes and return them to the pot.
- Add the butter and milk or cream to the potatoes and mash until smooth.
- Season with salt and pepper to taste. Keep warm.

3. Prepare the Onion Gravy:
   - In the same skillet used for cooking the sausages, melt the butter over medium heat.
   - Add the thinly sliced onions to the skillet and cook, stirring occasionally, until they are soft and caramelized, about 10-15 minutes.
   - Sprinkle the flour over the onions and stir to coat.
   - Gradually pour in the beef or chicken broth, stirring constantly to avoid lumps.
   - Bring the gravy to a simmer and cook until thickened, about 5-7 minutes.
   - Season with salt and pepper to taste.

4. Assemble and Serve:
   - To serve, spoon a generous portion of mashed potatoes onto each plate.
   - Place the cooked sausages on top of the mashed potatoes.
   - Ladle the onion gravy over the sausages and mashed potatoes.
   - Serve immediately, garnished with chopped parsley if desired.
   - Enjoy your comforting and delicious Bangers and Mash!

Ploughman's Lunch

Ingredients:

- Sliced crusty bread or rolls
- Assorted cheeses (such as cheddar, Stilton, or Red Leicester)
- Sliced ham or roast beef
- Pickles or chutney (such as Branston pickle or piccalilli)
- Hard-boiled eggs, halved
- Cherry tomatoes or sliced cucumber (optional)
- Mixed salad greens (such as lettuce or watercress)

Instructions:

1. Prepare the Ingredients:
    - Slice the crusty bread or rolls into thick slices.
    - Arrange the assorted cheeses on a serving platter. You can include a variety of cheeses to cater to different tastes.
    - Thinly slice the ham or roast beef and arrange it on the platter alongside the cheeses.
    - Place the pickles or chutney in small bowls or jars for serving.
    - Halve the hard-boiled eggs and set them aside.
    - If desired, include cherry tomatoes or sliced cucumber and mixed salad greens on the platter for added freshness and color.
2. Assemble the Ploughman's Lunch:
    - Arrange the sliced bread or rolls on a large serving platter or individual plates.
    - Place portions of cheese, ham or roast beef, pickles or chutney, and hard-boiled eggs alongside the bread.
    - Add cherry tomatoes or sliced cucumber and mixed salad greens to the platter for extra variety and visual appeal.
3. Serve:
    - Serve the Ploughman's Lunch immediately, allowing guests to help themselves to the various components.
    - Accompany the meal with condiments such as mustard or butter for the bread, and perhaps a side of ale or cider for a truly authentic experience.
    - Enjoy the simple yet satisfying flavors of this classic British dish, perfect for a leisurely lunch or casual gathering.

Toad in the Hole

Ingredients:

- 8 pork sausages (traditional British bangers)
- 2 tablespoons vegetable oil
- 1 cup (240ml) all-purpose flour
- 1/2 teaspoon salt
- 2 large eggs
- 1 cup (240ml) milk
- 1 tablespoon wholegrain mustard (optional)
- Freshly ground black pepper
- 2 tablespoons chopped fresh parsley (optional, for garnish)

Instructions:

1. Preheat the Oven:
    - Preheat your oven to 425°F (220°C). Place a 9x13-inch baking dish or a cast iron skillet in the oven to preheat as well.
2. Cook the Sausages:
    - While the oven is preheating, heat the vegetable oil in a large skillet over medium-high heat.
    - Add the sausages to the skillet and cook until they are browned on all sides, about 5 minutes. Remove from heat and set aside.
3. Make the Batter:
    - In a large mixing bowl, whisk together the flour and salt.
    - In a separate bowl, beat the eggs and then whisk in the milk until well combined.
    - Gradually add the egg and milk mixture to the flour mixture, whisking constantly until you have a smooth batter.
    - Stir in the wholegrain mustard, if using, and season with freshly ground black pepper.
4. Assemble and Bake:
    - Carefully remove the preheated baking dish or skillet from the oven.
    - Arrange the cooked sausages in the hot dish or skillet.
    - Pour the batter over the sausages, making sure they are evenly covered.
    - Return the dish or skillet to the oven and bake for 25-30 minutes, or until the batter is puffed up and golden brown.

5. Serve:
   - Once baked, remove the Toad in the Hole from the oven.
   - Sprinkle with chopped fresh parsley, if desired, and serve immediately.
   - Toad in the Hole is traditionally served with onion gravy and vegetables or mashed potatoes on the side.
   - Enjoy this comforting and hearty British classic!

Toad in the Hole is a delightful dish that combines the flavors of savory sausages with the light and airy texture of Yorkshire pudding batter. It's sure to be a hit at any meal!

Bubble and Squeak

Ingredients:

- 2 cups mashed potatoes (leftover or freshly made)
- 2 cups cooked cabbage (leftover or freshly cooked), finely chopped
- 1 small onion, finely chopped
- 2 tablespoons butter or vegetable oil
- Salt and pepper, to taste

Optional additions:

- Cooked carrots, peas, Brussels sprouts, or any other leftover vegetables you have on hand

Instructions:

1. Prepare the Ingredients:
    - If you don't have leftover mashed potatoes and cooked cabbage, you can prepare them fresh. Simply boil or steam potatoes until tender, mash them, and cook cabbage until softened. Let them cool before using.
2. Mix the Ingredients:
    - In a large mixing bowl, combine the mashed potatoes, chopped cabbage, and finely chopped onion. Mix well until all ingredients are evenly distributed.
3. Cook the Bubble and Squeak:
    - Heat the butter or vegetable oil in a large skillet over medium heat.
    - Add the potato and cabbage mixture to the skillet, spreading it out evenly.
    - Press the mixture down with a spatula to compact it into a large pancake shape.
    - Cook the Bubble and Squeak for 8-10 minutes on each side, or until golden brown and crispy. You can lift the edges occasionally to check the underside.
    - If the Bubble and Squeak is difficult to flip in one piece, you can divide it into smaller portions to make flipping easier.
4. Serve:

- Once both sides are golden and crispy, transfer the Bubble and Squeak to a serving plate.
- Season with salt and pepper to taste.
- Serve hot as a side dish for breakfast, lunch, or dinner.
- Bubble and Squeak pairs well with fried eggs, grilled sausages, or bacon.
- Enjoy the crispy and flavorful goodness of this traditional British dish made from leftover vegetables!

Bubble and Squeak is not only delicious but also a great way to use up leftover vegetables, reducing food waste while creating a tasty and satisfying meal.

Full English Breakfast

Ingredients:

- Bacon rashers (back bacon or streaky bacon)
- Pork sausages (traditional British bangers)
- Eggs (fried, poached, or scrambled)
- Black pudding slices (optional)
- Grilled tomatoes
- Sautéed mushrooms
- Baked beans
- Hash browns or fried potatoes
- Toast or fried bread
- Butter (for toast)
- Salt and pepper (for seasoning)

Instructions:

1. Cook the Bacon and Sausages:
    - In a large skillet or frying pan, cook the bacon rashers until crispy and golden brown.
    - In the same skillet, cook the pork sausages until they are browned and cooked through.
2. Prepare the Eggs:
    - While the bacon and sausages are cooking, prepare the eggs according to your preference. You can fry them, poach them, or scramble them.
3. Cook the Black Pudding (optional):
    - If using black pudding slices, cook them in a skillet or frying pan until heated through and crispy on the outside.
4. Grill the Tomatoes:
    - Preheat the grill (broiler) to high.
    - Cut the tomatoes in half and place them cut-side up on a baking sheet.
    - Grill the tomatoes until they are softened and slightly charred on top.
5. Sauté the Mushrooms:
    - In a separate skillet, sauté the mushrooms in butter until they are tender and golden brown.
6. Heat the Baked Beans:

- Heat the baked beans in a saucepan or microwave until they are hot.
7. Prepare the Hash Browns or Fried Potatoes:
    - If using hash browns, fry them in a skillet until crispy and golden brown on both sides. Alternatively, you can fry sliced potatoes until golden and crispy.
8. Toast or Fry the Bread:
    - Toast slices of bread or fry them in the leftover bacon fat until golden brown and crispy.
9. Assemble the Full English Breakfast:
    - Arrange all the cooked components on a large plate or individual serving plates.
    - Season everything with salt and pepper to taste.
    - Serve the Full English Breakfast with a cup of tea or coffee and your favorite condiments, such as ketchup or HP Sauce.

Enjoy your hearty and satisfying Full English Breakfast, a quintessential British morning meal that's perfect for starting the day off right!

Chicken Tikka Masala

Ingredients:

For the chicken marinade:

- 1.5 lbs (about 680g) boneless, skinless chicken breasts or thighs, cut into bite-sized pieces
- 1 cup plain yogurt
- 3 cloves garlic, minced
- 1 tablespoon grated ginger
- 1 tablespoon garam masala
- 1 teaspoon ground cumin
- 1 teaspoon ground coriander
- 1/2 teaspoon turmeric
- 1/2 teaspoon paprika
- 1/4 teaspoon cayenne pepper (adjust to taste)
- Salt and black pepper, to taste
- Juice of 1 lemon

For the sauce:

- 2 tablespoons vegetable oil or ghee
- 1 large onion, finely chopped
- 3 cloves garlic, minced
- 1 tablespoon grated ginger
- 1 tablespoon garam masala
- 1 teaspoon ground cumin
- 1 teaspoon ground coriander
- 1/2 teaspoon turmeric
- 1/2 teaspoon paprika
- 1/4 teaspoon cayenne pepper (adjust to taste)
- 1 can (14 oz/400g) diced tomatoes
- 1 cup heavy cream or coconut milk
- Salt and black pepper, to taste
- Fresh cilantro, chopped, for garnish
- Cooked rice or naan bread, for serving

Instructions:

1. Marinate the Chicken:
   - In a large bowl, combine the yogurt, minced garlic, grated ginger, garam masala, ground cumin, ground coriander, turmeric, paprika, cayenne pepper, salt, black pepper, and lemon juice.
   - Add the chicken pieces to the marinade and toss to coat evenly. Cover and refrigerate for at least 1 hour, or overnight for best results.
2. Cook the Chicken:
   - Preheat the grill or grill pan to medium-high heat.
   - Thread the marinated chicken pieces onto skewers and grill for 6-8 minutes on each side, or until cooked through and slightly charred. Alternatively, you can bake the chicken in a preheated oven at 400°F (200°C) for 20-25 minutes, or until cooked through.
   - Once cooked, remove the chicken from the skewers and set aside.
3. Prepare the Sauce:
   - In a large skillet or saucepan, heat the vegetable oil or ghee over medium heat.
   - Add the chopped onion and cook until softened and translucent, about 5 minutes.
   - Stir in the minced garlic and grated ginger, and cook for another 1-2 minutes until fragrant.
   - Add the garam masala, ground cumin, ground coriander, turmeric, paprika, and cayenne pepper. Cook, stirring constantly, for about 1 minute.
   - Pour in the diced tomatoes with their juices and simmer for 10-15 minutes, until the sauce has thickened slightly.
   - Stir in the heavy cream or coconut milk and simmer for an additional 5 minutes. Adjust seasoning with salt and pepper to taste.
4. Combine Chicken and Sauce:
   - Add the grilled chicken pieces to the sauce and simmer for a few more minutes to allow the flavors to meld together.
   - If the sauce is too thick, you can add a little water to reach your desired consistency.
5. Serve:
   - Garnish the Chicken Tikka Masala with freshly chopped cilantro.
   - Serve hot over cooked rice or with naan bread on the side.
   - Enjoy your homemade Chicken Tikka Masala!

This recipe yields a delicious and aromatic Chicken Tikka Masala that's perfect for sharing with family and friends. Adjust the spices according to your taste preferences for a milder or spicier dish.

Scotch Eggs

Ingredients:

- 6 large eggs
- 1 lb (450g) ground pork sausage meat (you can use flavored sausage if desired)
- Salt and pepper, to taste
- 1/2 teaspoon dried thyme
- 1/2 teaspoon dried sage
- 1/4 teaspoon ground nutmeg
- 1 cup all-purpose flour
- 2 large eggs, beaten
- 1 cup breadcrumbs (plain or seasoned)
- Vegetable oil, for frying

Instructions:

1. Boil the Eggs:
    - Place the eggs in a saucepan and cover them with cold water.
    - Bring the water to a boil over medium-high heat.
    - Once boiling, reduce the heat to low and simmer the eggs for 9-10 minutes.
    - After cooking, immediately transfer the eggs to a bowl of ice water to cool completely.
    - Once cooled, peel the eggs and set them aside.
2. Prepare the Sausage Mixture:
    - In a mixing bowl, combine the ground pork sausage meat with salt, pepper, dried thyme, dried sage, and ground nutmeg. Mix well until the seasonings are evenly distributed.
3. Wrap the Eggs:
    - Divide the sausage mixture into 6 equal portions.
    - Flatten each portion of sausage meat into a thin, round patty.
    - Place a peeled hard-boiled egg in the center of each sausage patty.
    - Gently mold the sausage meat around the egg, ensuring it is evenly coated and sealed.
4. Coat the Eggs:

- Prepare three shallow bowls: one with all-purpose flour, one with beaten eggs, and one with breadcrumbs.
- Roll each sausage-coated egg in the flour, shaking off any excess.
- Dip the floured egg into the beaten eggs, ensuring it is fully coated.
- Finally, roll the egg in the breadcrumbs until it is evenly covered. Press lightly to adhere the breadcrumbs.

5. Fry the Eggs:
   - Heat vegetable oil in a deep fryer or large skillet to 350°F (180°C).
   - Carefully place the coated eggs into the hot oil, working in batches if necessary to avoid overcrowding.
   - Fry the Scotch Eggs for 6-8 minutes, turning occasionally, until they are golden brown and crispy on all sides.
   - Once cooked, remove the Scotch Eggs from the oil using a slotted spoon and transfer them to a plate lined with paper towels to drain excess oil.

6. Serve:
   - Serve the Scotch Eggs warm or at room temperature.
   - They can be enjoyed on their own or with dipping sauces such as mustard or ketchup.
   - Scotch Eggs are perfect for picnics, parties, or as a delicious snack anytime!

Enjoy your homemade Scotch Eggs, a tasty and satisfying treat with a crispy exterior and flavorful sausage and egg interior.

Cornish Pasty

Ingredients:

For the pastry:

- 2 cups (250g) all-purpose flour
- 1/2 teaspoon salt
- 1/2 cup (115g) unsalted butter, chilled and cubed
- 1/4 cup (60ml) cold water

For the filling:

- 1 lb (450g) beef chuck steak, diced into small pieces
- 1 large potato, peeled and diced into small pieces
- 1 onion, finely chopped
- 1 carrot, peeled and diced into small pieces
- Salt and pepper, to taste
- Optional: 1 tablespoon Worcestershire sauce
- Optional: 1 tablespoon chopped fresh parsley

For assembly:

- 1 egg, beaten (for egg wash)
- Optional: extra flour for dusting

Instructions:

1. Prepare the Pastry:
    - In a large mixing bowl, combine the all-purpose flour and salt.
    - Add the chilled and cubed butter to the flour mixture.
    - Using your fingertips or a pastry cutter, rub the butter into the flour until the mixture resembles coarse breadcrumbs.

- Gradually add the cold water, a little at a time, and mix until a dough forms. Be careful not to overwork the dough.
- Shape the dough into a ball, wrap it in plastic wrap, and refrigerate for at least 30 minutes.

2. Prepare the Filling:
    - In a large mixing bowl, combine the diced beef, diced potato, chopped onion, and diced carrot.
    - Season the filling mixture with salt, pepper, and Worcestershire sauce, if using. Add chopped parsley for extra flavor if desired. Mix well to combine.
3. Assemble the Pasties:
    - Preheat your oven to 400°F (200°C) and line a baking sheet with parchment paper.
    - On a lightly floured surface, divide the chilled pastry dough into 4 equal portions.
    - Roll out each portion of dough into a circle, about 8-10 inches (20-25 cm) in diameter and 1/4 inch (6 mm) thick.
    - Divide the filling mixture equally among the pastry circles, placing it in the center of each circle.
4. Seal and Crimp the Edges:
    - Fold one half of each pastry circle over the filling to form a semi-circle shape.
    - Press the edges firmly together to seal the pasties.
    - Crimp the edges of the pasties using your fingers or a fork to create a decorative pattern and ensure a tight seal.
5. Bake the Pasties:
    - Place the sealed pasties on the prepared baking sheet.
    - Brush the tops of the pasties with beaten egg for a golden finish.
    - Using a sharp knife, make a small slit in the top of each pasty to allow steam to escape during baking.
    - Bake in the preheated oven for 35-40 minutes, or until the pasties are golden brown and cooked through.
6. Serve:
    - Remove the Cornish Pasties from the oven and let them cool slightly before serving.
    - Enjoy your homemade Cornish Pasties warm or at room temperature, as a hearty meal or snack.

Cornish Pasties are a delicious and satisfying meal that can be enjoyed hot or cold, making them perfect for picnics, lunches, or dinner.

Lancashire Hotpot

Ingredients:

- 1.5 lbs (about 680g) lamb shoulder or leg, trimmed and cut into chunks
- 2 tablespoons vegetable oil
- 2 large onions, sliced
- 2 carrots, sliced
- 2 celery stalks, sliced
- 2 tablespoons all-purpose flour
- 2 cups (480ml) beef or lamb broth
- 1 tablespoon Worcestershire sauce
- 1 tablespoon tomato paste
- 1 teaspoon dried thyme
- Salt and pepper, to taste
- 4 large potatoes, thinly sliced
- Butter, for greasing
- Fresh parsley, chopped (optional, for garnish)

Instructions:

1. Preheat the Oven:
    - Preheat your oven to 350°F (180°C).
2. Brown the Lamb:
    - Heat the vegetable oil in a large ovenproof pot or Dutch oven over medium-high heat.
    - Add the lamb chunks in batches and brown them on all sides. Remove the browned lamb from the pot and set aside.
3. Cook the Vegetables:
    - In the same pot, add the sliced onions, carrots, and celery. Cook until softened, about 5-7 minutes.
4. Make the Gravy:
    - Sprinkle the flour over the cooked vegetables and stir to coat.
    - Gradually pour in the beef or lamb broth, stirring constantly to prevent lumps from forming.
    - Stir in the Worcestershire sauce, tomato paste, dried thyme, salt, and pepper.

5. Assemble the Hotpot:
    - Return the browned lamb to the pot and stir to combine with the vegetables and gravy.
    - Arrange the thinly sliced potatoes on top of the lamb mixture, overlapping them slightly.
    - Season the potatoes with salt and pepper, and dot with small pieces of butter for extra richness.
6. Bake the Hotpot:
    - Cover the pot with a lid or foil and transfer it to the preheated oven.
    - Bake for 2 to 2.5 hours, or until the lamb is tender and the potatoes are golden brown and crispy on top.
7. Serve:
    - Remove the Lancashire Hotpot from the oven and let it rest for a few minutes.
    - Garnish with chopped fresh parsley, if desired, before serving.
    - Serve hot, straight from the pot, with crusty bread or green vegetables on the side.

Lancashire Hotpot is a comforting and flavorful dish that's perfect for colder weather.

Enjoy the tender lamb, rich gravy, and crispy potatoes in this classic British recipe.

Welsh Rarebit

Ingredients:

- 2 tablespoons unsalted butter
- 2 tablespoons all-purpose flour
- 1 cup (240ml) milk
- 2 cups (200g) grated sharp cheddar cheese
- 1 teaspoon Dijon mustard
- 1 teaspoon Worcestershire sauce
- 1/4 teaspoon cayenne pepper (optional)
- Salt and pepper, to taste
- 4-6 slices of bread (traditionally white bread or sourdough)
- Optional: sliced tomatoes, crispy bacon, or cooked ham for serving

Instructions:

1. Prepare the Cheese Sauce:
    - In a saucepan, melt the butter over medium heat.
    - Stir in the flour and cook, stirring constantly, for 1-2 minutes to make a roux.
    - Gradually whisk in the milk, a little at a time, until smooth and thickened.
    - Reduce the heat to low and add the grated cheddar cheese to the sauce, stirring until melted and well combined.
    - Stir in the Dijon mustard, Worcestershire sauce, and cayenne pepper (if using).
    - Season the cheese sauce with salt and pepper to taste. Keep warm while you prepare the toast.
2. Toast the Bread:
    - Toast the slices of bread until golden brown and crispy. You can use a toaster or toast them under the broiler in the oven.
3. Assemble and Serve:
    - Place the toasted bread slices on a baking sheet or ovenproof dish.
    - Pour the warm cheese sauce over the toasted bread, spreading it evenly to cover each slice.
    - If desired, top each Welsh Rarebit with sliced tomatoes, crispy bacon, or cooked ham for extra flavor and texture.

- Place the Welsh Rarebit under the broiler for 1-2 minutes, or until the cheese sauce is bubbly and slightly golden on top.
- Serve immediately, garnished with fresh parsley if desired.
- Enjoy your homemade Welsh Rarebit as a comforting and satisfying meal!

Welsh Rarebit is a versatile dish that can be enjoyed on its own or paired with a side salad or soup for a more substantial meal. It's a classic comfort food that's sure to be a hit with cheese lovers!

Steak and Kidney Pie

Ingredients:

For the filling:

- 1 lb (about 450g) beef steak, cubed
- 8 oz (about 225g) beef kidney, cleaned and diced
- 2 tablespoons all-purpose flour
- Salt and pepper, to taste
- 2 tablespoons vegetable oil
- 1 onion, chopped
- 2 cloves garlic, minced
- 2 carrots, diced
- 2 celery stalks, diced
- 1 tablespoon tomato paste
- 1 tablespoon Worcestershire sauce
- 1 teaspoon dried thyme
- 1 teaspoon dried rosemary
- 1 cup (240ml) beef broth
- 1/2 cup (120ml) red wine (optional)
- 1 bay leaf

For the pastry:

- 2 sheets of store-bought puff pastry, thawed if frozen
- 1 egg, beaten (for egg wash)

Instructions:

1. Prepare the Filling:
    - In a bowl, toss the cubed beef steak and diced kidney with the all-purpose flour, salt, and pepper until well coated.
    - Heat the vegetable oil in a large skillet or Dutch oven over medium-high heat.

- Add the floured beef steak and kidney to the skillet and cook until browned on all sides. Remove from the skillet and set aside.
- In the same skillet, add the chopped onion, minced garlic, diced carrots, and diced celery. Cook until the vegetables are softened, about 5-7 minutes.
- Stir in the tomato paste, Worcestershire sauce, dried thyme, and dried rosemary, coating the vegetables evenly.
- Return the browned beef steak and kidney to the skillet. Pour in the beef broth and red wine (if using). Add the bay leaf.
- Bring the mixture to a simmer, then reduce the heat to low. Cover and cook for 1.5 to 2 hours, or until the beef is tender and the flavors have melded together. Stir occasionally. Remove the bay leaf before assembling the pie.

2. Preheat the Oven:
    - Preheat your oven to 400°F (200°C).
3. Assemble the Pie:
    - Roll out one sheet of puff pastry on a lightly floured surface to fit the bottom and sides of a pie dish. Line the pie dish with the pastry, leaving any excess hanging over the edges.
    - Pour the cooked steak and kidney filling into the pastry-lined pie dish.
    - Roll out the second sheet of puff pastry to fit the top of the pie dish. Place it over the filling.
    - Trim any excess pastry and crimp the edges to seal the pie.
    - Cut a few slits in the top pastry to allow steam to escape during baking.
    - Brush the top of the pastry with beaten egg for a golden finish.
4. Bake the Pie:
    - Place the assembled pie on a baking sheet to catch any drips.
    - Bake in the preheated oven for 25-30 minutes, or until the pastry is puffed and golden brown.
5. Serve:
    - Remove the steak and kidney pie from the oven and let it cool slightly before serving.
    - Serve slices of the pie with your favorite sides, such as mashed potatoes and steamed vegetables.
    - Enjoy this comforting and flavorful British classic!

Chicken and Leek Pie

Ingredients:

For the filling:

- 2 tablespoons butter
- 2 leeks, washed and sliced
- 2 cloves garlic, minced
- 1 lb (about 450g) boneless, skinless chicken breasts or thighs, cut into bite-sized pieces
- 2 tablespoons all-purpose flour
- 1 cup (240ml) chicken broth
- 1 cup (240ml) heavy cream
- 1 teaspoon dried thyme
- Salt and pepper, to taste
- 1 cup frozen peas (optional)

For the pastry:

- 2 sheets of store-bought puff pastry, thawed if frozen
- 1 egg, beaten (for egg wash)

Instructions:

1. Prepare the Filling:
    - In a large skillet or saucepan, melt the butter over medium heat.
    - Add the sliced leeks and minced garlic to the skillet. Cook, stirring occasionally, until the leeks are soft and translucent, about 5-7 minutes.
    - Add the diced chicken to the skillet and cook until browned on all sides.
    - Sprinkle the flour over the chicken and leeks, stirring to coat evenly.
    - Gradually pour in the chicken broth and heavy cream, stirring constantly to avoid lumps.
    - Stir in the dried thyme, salt, and pepper. Bring the mixture to a simmer and cook for 5-7 minutes, or until thickened.

- If using, add the frozen peas to the skillet and cook for an additional 2-3 minutes, until heated through. Remove from heat and let the filling cool slightly.
2. Preheat the Oven:
    - Preheat your oven to 400°F (200°C).
3. Assemble the Pie:
    - Roll out one sheet of puff pastry on a lightly floured surface to fit the bottom and sides of a pie dish. Line the pie dish with the pastry, leaving any excess hanging over the edges.
    - Pour the slightly cooled chicken and leek filling into the pastry-lined pie dish.
    - Roll out the second sheet of puff pastry to fit the top of the pie dish. Place it over the filling.
    - Trim any excess pastry and crimp the edges to seal the pie.
    - Cut a few slits in the top pastry to allow steam to escape during baking.
    - Brush the top of the pastry with beaten egg for a golden finish.
4. Bake the Pie:
    - Place the assembled pie on a baking sheet to catch any drips.
    - Bake in the preheated oven for 25-30 minutes, or until the pastry is puffed and golden brown.
5. Serve:
    - Remove the chicken and leek pie from the oven and let it cool slightly before serving.
    - Serve slices of the pie with your favorite sides, such as mashed potatoes and steamed vegetables.
    - Enjoy this comforting and flavorful British classic!

Pork Pie

Ingredients:

For the pastry:

- 2 1/2 cups (300g) all-purpose flour
- 1 teaspoon salt
- 1/2 cup (115g) cold unsalted butter, cut into cubes
- 1/4 cup (60g) cold lard or vegetable shortening
- 6-8 tablespoons ice water

For the filling:

- 1 lb (450g) ground pork
- 1/2 lb (225g) pork sausage meat
- 1 onion, finely chopped
- 2 cloves garlic, minced
- 1 teaspoon dried sage
- 1/2 teaspoon dried thyme
- 1/2 teaspoon ground black pepper
- 1/4 teaspoon ground nutmeg
- Salt, to taste
- 1/4 cup (60ml) chicken or pork stock

Instructions:

1. Make the Pastry:
    - In a large mixing bowl, combine the flour and salt.
    - Add the cold butter and lard or vegetable shortening to the flour mixture.
    - Using a pastry blender or your fingertips, rub the fat into the flour until the mixture resembles coarse breadcrumbs.
    - Gradually add the ice water, a tablespoon at a time, mixing with a fork until the dough comes together.
    - Shape the dough into a ball, wrap it in plastic wrap, and refrigerate for at least 30 minutes.

2. Prepare the Filling:
   - In a large skillet, cook the ground pork and pork sausage meat over medium heat until browned and cooked through.
   - Add the chopped onion and minced garlic to the skillet and cook until softened, about 5 minutes.
   - Stir in the dried sage, dried thyme, ground black pepper, ground nutmeg, and salt to taste.
   - Pour in the chicken or pork stock and simmer for a few minutes until the liquid is absorbed. Remove from heat and let the filling cool slightly.
3. Assemble the Pie:
   - Preheat your oven to 375°F (190°C).
   - Divide the pastry dough into two portions, one slightly larger than the other.
   - Roll out the larger portion of dough on a lightly floured surface to fit the base and sides of a 9-inch (23cm) pie dish or cake pan.
   - Press the pastry dough into the bottom and sides of the pie dish, leaving any excess hanging over the edges.
   - Spoon the cooled pork filling into the pastry-lined dish, spreading it out evenly.
   - Roll out the remaining portion of dough to fit the top of the pie.
   - Place the pastry over the filling, sealing the edges with the bottom crust. Trim any excess pastry and crimp the edges to seal.
4. Bake the Pie:
   - Using a sharp knife, make a few slits in the top pastry to allow steam to escape during baking.
   - Bake the pork pie in the preheated oven for 45-50 minutes, or until the pastry is golden brown and crisp.
5. Serve:
   - Allow the pork pie to cool slightly before slicing and serving.
   - Serve slices of the pie warm or at room temperature, accompanied by pickles, chutney, or mustard.
   - Enjoy the delicious flavors of this classic British pork pie!

Homemade pork pie is a wonderful dish to serve as part of a picnic, buffet, or as a main course with a side salad. It's a comforting and flavorful dish that's sure to be a hit with family and friends.

Black Pudding

Ingredients:

- 1 lb (about 450g) fresh pork blood (can be obtained from a butcher)
- 1 cup (100g) steel-cut oats or barley groats
- 1 large onion, finely chopped
- 1/4 lb (about 115g) pork fatback or pork belly, finely chopped
- 1 teaspoon salt
- 1/2 teaspoon ground black pepper
- 1/2 teaspoon ground allspice
- 1/2 teaspoon ground nutmeg
- 1/2 teaspoon dried thyme
- 1/4 teaspoon ground cloves
- 1/4 teaspoon ground mace
- Hog casings (optional, for casing the pudding)

Instructions:

1. Prepare the Ingredients:
    - If using hog casings, soak them in cold water for at least 30 minutes to soften.
    - In a saucepan, bring water to a boil and blanch the steel-cut oats or barley groats for 5 minutes. Drain and set aside.
2. Mix the Ingredients:
    - In a large mixing bowl, combine the fresh pork blood, blanched oats or barley groats, finely chopped onion, finely chopped pork fatback or pork belly, salt, black pepper, allspice, nutmeg, thyme, cloves, and mace. Mix until well combined.
3. Stuff the Casings (optional):
    - If using hog casings, fit a sausage stuffer with the hog casings and fill them with the black pudding mixture. Tie the ends of the casings with kitchen twine to secure.
4. Cook the Black Pudding:
    - Bring a large pot of water to a simmer. If using cased black pudding, prick the casings with a needle to prevent bursting during cooking.

- Carefully place the black pudding, whether cased or not, into the simmering water.
- Cook for 1 to 1.5 hours, maintaining a gentle simmer, until the black pudding is firm and cooked through.

5. Cool and Serve:
    - Once cooked, remove the black pudding from the water and let it cool slightly.
    - If using cased black pudding, remove the casings before serving.
    - Slice the black pudding into rounds and serve warm or at room temperature.

Homemade black pudding is a versatile ingredient that can be enjoyed on its own, fried until crispy and served as part of a full breakfast, or used in various recipes. Adjust the seasoning to your taste preferences for a unique and flavorful blood sausage.

Sunday Roast (with Yorkshire Pudding)

Ingredients:

For the roast:

- 1 (3-4 lb) bone-in beef, pork, or lamb roast
- Salt and pepper, to taste
- 2 tablespoons vegetable oil or beef drippings

For the Yorkshire pudding:

- 1 cup (120g) all-purpose flour
- 1 cup (240ml) whole milk
- 4 large eggs
- 1/2 teaspoon salt
- Vegetable oil or beef drippings, for greasing

For the roast potatoes:

- 2 lbs (about 900g) potatoes, peeled and cut into chunks
- 2-3 tablespoons vegetable oil or beef drippings
- Salt and pepper, to taste

For the gravy:

- Pan drippings from the roast
- 2 tablespoons all-purpose flour
- 2 cups (480ml) beef or chicken broth
- Salt and pepper, to taste

For the vegetables:

- Carrots, parsnips, and Brussels sprouts, peeled and trimmed
- Olive oil
- Salt and pepper, to taste

Instructions:

1. Prepare the Roast:
    - Preheat your oven to 375°F (190°C).
    - Season the roast generously with salt and pepper.
    - Heat the vegetable oil or beef drippings in a roasting pan over medium-high heat on the stovetop.
    - Sear the roast on all sides until browned.
2. Roast the Meat:
    - Transfer the roasting pan to the preheated oven.
    - Roast the meat until it reaches your desired level of doneness:
        - For beef: 20 minutes per pound for medium-rare, or until the internal temperature reaches 135°F (57°C).
        - For pork: 25 minutes per pound, or until the internal temperature reaches 145°F (63°C).
        - For lamb: 25 minutes per pound for medium-rare, or until the internal temperature reaches 135°F (57°C).
    - Once cooked, remove the roast from the oven and let it rest for 15-20 minutes before carving.
3. Prepare the Yorkshire Pudding Batter:
    - In a mixing bowl, whisk together the flour, milk, eggs, and salt until smooth.
    - Let the batter rest at room temperature for at least 30 minutes.
4. Make the Yorkshire Pudding:
    - Increase the oven temperature to 425°F (220°C).
    - Pour a small amount of vegetable oil or beef drippings into each well of a muffin tin or a Yorkshire pudding pan.
    - Place the pan in the oven for 5 minutes to heat the oil.
    - Carefully pour the Yorkshire pudding batter into the hot oil, filling each well about halfway.
    - Bake for 20-25 minutes, or until the Yorkshire puddings are puffed and golden brown.
5. Roast the Potatoes:
    - While the Yorkshire pudding is baking, parboil the potatoes in a large pot of salted water for 5-7 minutes, until slightly softened.
    - Drain the potatoes and toss them with vegetable oil or beef drippings, salt, and pepper.

- Arrange the potatoes in a single layer on a baking sheet and roast in the oven for 30-40 minutes, or until crispy and golden brown.
6. Prepare the Gravy:
    - While the roast is resting, make the gravy by deglazing the roasting pan with a little water or broth, scraping up any browned bits.
    - Sprinkle the flour over the pan drippings and cook, stirring constantly, for 1-2 minutes.
    - Gradually whisk in the beef or chicken broth until smooth.
    - Simmer the gravy until thickened, then season with salt and pepper to taste.
7. Roast the Vegetables:
    - Toss the prepared vegetables with olive oil, salt, and pepper.
    - Roast in the oven for 20-25 minutes, or until tender and caramelized.
8. Serve:
    - Carve the roast and serve it with the Yorkshire pudding, roast potatoes, roasted vegetables, and gravy.
    - Enjoy your delicious Sunday roast with all the trimmings!

A Sunday roast with Yorkshire pudding is a hearty and comforting meal that's perfect for gathering with family and friends. Customize it with your favorite meats, vegetables, and gravy for a memorable dining experience.

Cottage Pie

Ingredients:

For the filling:

- 1 lb (450g) ground beef (or lamb)
- 1 onion, chopped
- 2 carrots, diced
- 2 celery stalks, diced
- 2 cloves garlic, minced
- 2 tablespoons tomato paste
- 1 tablespoon Worcestershire sauce
- 1 cup (240ml) beef or vegetable broth
- 1 teaspoon dried thyme
- Salt and pepper, to taste
- 1 cup frozen peas (optional)
- 2 tablespoons all-purpose flour (for thickening, optional)

For the mashed potatoes:

- 2 lbs (about 900g) potatoes, peeled and cut into chunks
- 4 tablespoons unsalted butter
- 1/2 cup (120ml) milk or cream
- Salt and pepper, to taste

Instructions:

1. Prepare the Filling:
    - Preheat your oven to 375°F (190°C).
    - In a large skillet or saucepan, cook the ground beef over medium heat until browned. Drain excess fat if needed.
    - Add the chopped onion, diced carrots, diced celery, and minced garlic to the skillet. Cook until the vegetables are softened, about 5-7 minutes.
    - Stir in the tomato paste, Worcestershire sauce, dried thyme, salt, and pepper.

- Pour in the beef or vegetable broth and bring the mixture to a simmer. Cook for 10-15 minutes, stirring occasionally, until the filling has thickened. If desired, sprinkle the flour over the filling to help thicken it further.
- If using frozen peas, stir them into the filling during the last few minutes of cooking. Remove from heat and set aside.

2. Prepare the Mashed Potatoes:
   - While the filling is cooking, place the potato chunks in a large pot and cover with cold water. Bring to a boil and cook until the potatoes are fork-tender, about 15-20 minutes.
   - Drain the cooked potatoes and return them to the pot. Add the butter, milk or cream, salt, and pepper.
   - Mash the potatoes with a potato masher or fork until smooth and creamy. Adjust seasoning to taste.

3. Assemble the Cottage Pie:
   - Transfer the cooked filling to a baking dish and spread it out evenly.
   - Spoon the mashed potatoes over the filling, spreading them out to cover the entire surface.
   - Use a fork to create a decorative pattern on top of the mashed potatoes.

4. Bake the Cottage Pie:
   - Place the assembled cottage pie in the preheated oven and bake for 25-30 minutes, or until the mashed potatoes are golden brown and the filling is bubbling around the edges.

5. Serve:
   - Remove the cottage pie from the oven and let it cool slightly before serving.
   - Serve slices of the cottage pie warm, accompanied by your favorite sides such as steamed vegetables or a green salad.
   - Enjoy the comforting flavors of this classic British dish!

Cottage pie is a hearty and satisfying meal that's perfect for a cozy family dinner. It's also a great way to use up leftover mashed potatoes and vegetables. Feel free to customize the filling with your favorite herbs and spices for a personalized touch.

Spotted Dick

Ingredients:

- 1 cup (150g) all-purpose flour
- 1/2 cup (100g) shredded suet (vegetarian suet can be used)
- 1/2 cup (100g) granulated sugar
- 1/2 cup (75g) dried currants or raisins
- Zest of 1 lemon (optional)
- 1 teaspoon baking powder
- Pinch of salt
- Milk or water, as needed

For the custard (optional):

- 2 cups (480ml) whole milk
- 4 large egg yolks
- 1/4 cup (50g) granulated sugar
- 2 tablespoons cornstarch
- 1 teaspoon vanilla extract

Instructions:

1. Prepare the Steamed Pudding:
     - In a large mixing bowl, combine the all-purpose flour, shredded suet, granulated sugar, dried currants or raisins, lemon zest (if using), baking powder, and a pinch of salt.
     - Gradually add enough milk or water to form a soft, sticky dough. Be careful not to overmix.
     - Grease a pudding basin or heatproof bowl with butter or non-stick cooking spray.
     - Spoon the spotted dick mixture into the greased basin, filling it about three-quarters full.
2. Steam the Pudding:
     - Cover the pudding basin with a double layer of parchment paper or aluminum foil, securing it tightly with kitchen twine.

- Place the pudding basin in a large pot and add enough boiling water to come halfway up the sides of the basin.
- Cover the pot with a tight-fitting lid and steam the pudding over low heat for 1.5 to 2 hours, or until firm and cooked through. Check the water level occasionally and top up with boiling water as needed.

3. Make the Custard (optional):
   - In a saucepan, heat the whole milk over medium heat until it just begins to simmer.
   - In a separate bowl, whisk together the egg yolks, granulated sugar, cornstarch, and vanilla extract until smooth and creamy.
   - Slowly pour the hot milk into the egg mixture, whisking constantly to prevent curdling.
   - Return the custard mixture to the saucepan and cook over low heat, stirring constantly, until thickened and smooth. Remove from heat and let cool slightly.

4. Serve:
   - Once the spotted dick is cooked, carefully remove it from the pudding basin and transfer it to a serving plate.
   - Slice the spotted dick into thick slices and serve warm, drizzled with custard sauce if desired.

Spotted dick is a comforting and nostalgic dessert that's perfect for a cozy night in.

Enjoy its rich, fruity flavors with a dollop of custard for a truly traditional British treat.

Sticky Toffee Pudding

Ingredients:

For the pudding:

- 1 cup (200g) chopped dates
- 1 cup (240ml) boiling water
- 1 teaspoon baking soda
- 1 3/4 cups (220g) all-purpose flour
- 1 teaspoon baking powder
- 1/2 teaspoon salt
- 1/2 cup (115g) unsalted butter, softened
- 3/4 cup (150g) granulated sugar
- 2 large eggs
- 1 teaspoon vanilla extract

For the toffee sauce:

- 1 cup (200g) dark brown sugar
- 1/2 cup (115g) unsalted butter
- 3/4 cup (180ml) heavy cream
- Pinch of salt
- 1 teaspoon vanilla extract

Instructions:

1. Prepare the Pudding:
    - Preheat your oven to 350°F (175°C). Grease a 9x9-inch (23x23cm) baking dish.
    - In a bowl, combine the chopped dates and boiling water. Stir in the baking soda and let it sit for 5-10 minutes to soften the dates.
    - In a separate bowl, whisk together the all-purpose flour, baking powder, and salt.
    - In another bowl, cream together the softened butter and granulated sugar until light and fluffy.

- Beat in the eggs, one at a time, followed by the vanilla extract.
- Gradually add the flour mixture to the butter mixture, mixing until just combined.
- Fold in the softened dates and any remaining liquid.
- Pour the batter into the prepared baking dish, spreading it out evenly.

2. Bake the Pudding:
    - Bake in the preheated oven for 30-35 minutes, or until the pudding is set and a toothpick inserted into the center comes out clean.
3. Prepare the Toffee Sauce:
    - While the pudding is baking, prepare the toffee sauce. In a saucepan, combine the dark brown sugar, unsalted butter, heavy cream, and salt.
    - Cook over medium heat, stirring constantly, until the sugar has dissolved and the mixture is smooth.
    - Let the sauce simmer gently for 5-7 minutes, stirring occasionally, until slightly thickened.
    - Remove the saucepan from heat and stir in the vanilla extract.
4. Serve:
    - Once the pudding is baked, remove it from the oven and poke holes all over the surface with a skewer or fork.
    - Pour half of the warm toffee sauce over the hot pudding, allowing it to soak in.
    - Serve slices of the sticky toffee pudding warm, drizzled with extra toffee sauce and perhaps a scoop of vanilla ice cream or a dollop of whipped cream.

Sticky toffee pudding is a decadent and indulgent dessert that's perfect for special occasions or a cozy night in. Enjoy its rich, moist texture and irresistible toffee flavor!

Trifle

Ingredients:

- 1 store-bought sponge cake or 1-2 packages of ladyfingers
- 1/2 cup (120ml) sherry or fruit juice (optional)
- 2 cups (480ml) custard (homemade or store-bought)
- 2 cups (480ml) whipped cream
- Fresh fruit (such as berries, sliced strawberries, or canned fruit like peaches or pineapple)
- Jam or fruit preserves (optional)
- Sliced almonds or grated chocolate for garnish (optional)

Instructions:

1. Prepare the Sponge Cake or Ladyfingers:
   - If using a sponge cake, slice it into thin layers. If using ladyfingers, arrange them in the bottom of a trifle dish or a large glass bowl.
2. Soak the Cake or Ladyfingers (optional):
   - If desired, drizzle the sponge cake or ladyfingers with sherry or fruit juice to moisten them. This step is optional and can be omitted for a non-alcoholic version.
3. Layer the Trifle:
   - Spread a layer of custard over the soaked cake or ladyfingers.
   - Add a layer of fresh fruit on top of the custard. You can also add a layer of jam or fruit preserves for extra flavor if desired.
   - Repeat the layers as desired, ending with a layer of whipped cream on top.
4. Garnish:
   - Garnish the top of the trifle with sliced almonds or grated chocolate for added texture and decoration.
5. Chill:
   - Cover the trifle with plastic wrap and refrigerate for at least 4 hours, or preferably overnight, to allow the flavors to meld together and the dessert to set.
6. Serve:
   - Before serving, remove the trifle from the refrigerator and let it sit at room temperature for about 15 minutes to slightly soften.

- Serve the trifle chilled, scooping out portions into individual dessert bowls or glasses.

Trifle is a versatile dessert that can be customized with different flavors of custard, fruit, and cake to suit your preferences. Experiment with various combinations to create your own signature trifle recipe!

Eton Mess

Ingredients:

- 1 cup (240ml) heavy cream
- 2 tablespoons powdered sugar (or to taste)
- 1 teaspoon vanilla extract
- 4-6 meringue nests or 1 cup crushed meringue
- 2 cups (about 300g) fresh strawberries, hulled and sliced
- Additional berries for garnish (optional)
- Mint leaves for garnish (optional)

Instructions:

1. Whip the Cream:
    - In a large mixing bowl, whip the heavy cream until stiff peaks form. Be careful not to over-whip.
    - Add the powdered sugar and vanilla extract to the whipped cream, and gently fold them in until incorporated. Taste and adjust sweetness if necessary.
2. Prepare the Meringue:
    - If using meringue nests, crush them into small pieces. Alternatively, you can make homemade meringue and crush it into bite-sized chunks.
3. Assemble the Eton Mess:
    - In serving glasses or bowls, layer the whipped cream, crushed meringue, and sliced strawberries. Repeat the layers until the glasses are filled, ending with a dollop of whipped cream on top.
4. Garnish:
    - Garnish the Eton Mess with additional fresh berries and mint leaves if desired.
5. Serve:
    - Serve the Eton Mess immediately, as the meringue will soften if left to sit for too long.
    - Enjoy this delightful and refreshing dessert!

Eton Mess is a light and airy dessert that's perfect for summer gatherings or any occasion when you want something sweet and satisfying. Feel free to customize it by using different types of berries or adding a drizzle of fruit coulis for extra flavor.

Crumpets

Ingredients:

- 2 cups (250g) all-purpose flour
- 1 teaspoon active dry yeast
- 1 teaspoon sugar
- 1 teaspoon salt
- 1 cup (240ml) warm milk
- 1/2 cup (120ml) warm water
- 1/2 teaspoon baking soda
- Vegetable oil or butter, for cooking

Instructions:

1. Prepare the Batter:
    - In a large mixing bowl, combine the all-purpose flour, active dry yeast, sugar, and salt.
    - Gradually add the warm milk and warm water to the dry ingredients, stirring until a smooth batter forms. The batter should be thick but pourable.
    - Cover the bowl with a clean kitchen towel or plastic wrap and let the batter rest in a warm, draft-free place for about 1 hour, or until it becomes frothy and bubbly.
2. Prepare the Crumpet Rings:
    - Lightly grease the insides of crumpet rings or metal biscuit cutters with vegetable oil or butter. If you don't have crumpet rings, you can use clean, empty tuna cans with the tops and bottoms removed.
3. Cook the Crumpets:
    - Heat a non-stick skillet or griddle over medium-low heat. Place the greased crumpet rings onto the skillet.
    - Once the skillet is hot, pour a small amount of batter into each crumpet ring, filling them about halfway. The batter will spread out slightly as it cooks.
    - Cook the crumpets for 5-6 minutes, or until bubbles form on the surface and the edges start to set.

- Carefully remove the crumpet rings using tongs or oven mitts. If the crumpets stick to the rings, gently loosen them with a knife or spatula.
- Flip the crumpets over and cook for an additional 2-3 minutes, or until golden brown and cooked through.

4. Serve:
    - Transfer the cooked crumpets to a wire rack to cool slightly.
    - Toast the crumpets until golden brown on both sides.
    - Serve the warm crumpets with butter, jam, honey, or your favorite spread.
    - Enjoy these delicious homemade crumpets for breakfast or as a tasty snack!

Homemade crumpets are a delightful treat, perfect for enjoying with a cup of tea or coffee. Experiment with toppings and enjoy the fluffy, golden goodness of freshly made crumpets anytime!

Scones with Clotted Cream and Jam

Ingredients:

For the scones:

- 2 cups (250g) all-purpose flour
- 1/4 cup (50g) granulated sugar
- 1 tablespoon baking powder
- 1/2 teaspoon salt
- 1/3 cup (75g) cold unsalted butter, cut into small cubes
- 2/3 cup (160ml) milk
- 1 large egg
- 1 teaspoon vanilla extract

For serving:

- Clotted cream
- Strawberry jam or raspberry jam

Instructions:

1. Preheat the Oven:
    - Preheat your oven to 400°F (200°C). Line a baking sheet with parchment paper or lightly grease it.
2. Prepare the Scone Dough:
    - In a large mixing bowl, whisk together the all-purpose flour, granulated sugar, baking powder, and salt.
    - Add the cold cubed butter to the flour mixture. Using your fingertips or a pastry cutter, rub the butter into the flour until the mixture resembles coarse crumbs with some pea-sized pieces of butter remaining.
    - In a separate bowl, whisk together the milk, egg, and vanilla extract.
    - Pour the wet ingredients into the dry ingredients and stir until the dough comes together. Be careful not to overmix.
3. Shape and Cut the Scones:
    - Transfer the dough onto a lightly floured surface. Gently pat the dough into a circle about 3/4-inch (2cm) thick.

- Using a floured round cutter, cut out scones from the dough and place them onto the prepared baking sheet, leaving some space between each scone.
- Gather any remaining dough scraps, pat them together, and cut out more scones until all the dough is used.
4. Bake the Scones:
    - Place the baking sheet in the preheated oven and bake the scones for 12-15 minutes, or until they are golden brown and cooked through.
    - Remove the scones from the oven and transfer them to a wire rack to cool slightly.
5. Serve with Clotted Cream and Jam:
    - Split the warm scones in half horizontally using a serrated knife.
    - Spread a generous dollop of clotted cream onto each half of the scones.
    - Top the clotted cream with a spoonful of strawberry jam or raspberry jam.
    - Place the top halves of the scones back on top of the jam to create sandwiches.
    - Serve the scones with clotted cream and jam alongside a pot of hot tea or coffee for a delightful treat!

Enjoy these freshly baked scones with indulgent clotted cream and sweet, tangy jam for a classic British afternoon tea experience.

Fish Pie

Ingredients:

For the mashed potato topping:

- 2 lbs (about 900g) potatoes, peeled and cut into chunks
- 4 tablespoons unsalted butter
- 1/2 cup (120ml) milk or cream
- Salt and pepper, to taste

For the fish filling:

- 1 lb (about 450g) mixed white fish fillets (such as cod, haddock, or pollock), cut into chunks
- 1/2 lb (about 225g) smoked haddock fillets, cut into chunks (optional)
- 1/2 lb (about 225g) raw shrimp or prawns, peeled and deveined
- 1 onion, finely chopped
- 2 carrots, diced
- 2 celery stalks, diced
- 2 tablespoons unsalted butter
- 3 tablespoons all-purpose flour
- 2 cups (480ml) fish or vegetable broth
- 1 cup (240ml) milk or cream
- 1/4 cup (60ml) dry white wine (optional)
- 1/4 cup (60g) frozen peas
- 2 tablespoons chopped fresh parsley
- Salt and pepper, to taste

Instructions:

1. Prepare the Mashed Potato Topping:
    - Place the potato chunks in a large pot of salted water. Bring to a boil and cook until the potatoes are fork-tender, about 15-20 minutes.
    - Drain the cooked potatoes and return them to the pot. Add the butter, milk or cream, salt, and pepper.

- Mash the potatoes until smooth and creamy. Adjust seasoning to taste.
2. Prepare the Fish Filling:
    - Preheat your oven to 375°F (190°C).
    - In a large skillet, melt the butter over medium heat. Add the chopped onion, diced carrots, and diced celery. Cook until the vegetables are softened, about 5-7 minutes.
    - Stir in the all-purpose flour and cook for 1-2 minutes, stirring constantly.
    - Gradually pour in the fish or vegetable broth, milk or cream, and white wine (if using), stirring constantly to prevent lumps from forming.
    - Bring the mixture to a simmer and cook for 5-7 minutes, or until thickened, stirring occasionally.
    - Stir in the chopped parsley, frozen peas, and salt and pepper to taste.
    - Add the chunks of white fish, smoked haddock (if using), and raw shrimp or prawns to the skillet. Stir gently to combine and cook for an additional 3-4 minutes, or until the fish is just cooked through.
3. Assemble the Fish Pie:
    - Transfer the fish filling to a baking dish or individual ramekins, spreading it out evenly.
    - Spoon the mashed potato topping over the fish filling, spreading it out to cover the entire surface.
4. Bake the Fish Pie:
    - Place the assembled fish pie in the preheated oven and bake for 25-30 minutes, or until the mashed potato topping is golden brown and the filling is bubbling around the edges.
5. Serve:
    - Remove the fish pie from the oven and let it cool slightly before serving.
    - Serve slices of the fish pie warm, accompanied by steamed vegetables or a green salad, if desired.

Fish pie is a comforting and satisfying dish that's perfect for a cozy dinner. Enjoy the creamy sauce, flaky fish, and buttery mashed potato topping in every delicious bite!

Cock-a-Leekie Soup

Ingredients:

- 1 whole chicken (about 3-4 lbs), rinsed and patted dry
- 2 large leeks, white and light green parts only, sliced
- 2 carrots, diced
- 2 celery stalks, diced
- 1 onion, diced
- 2 cloves garlic, minced
- 1/2 cup pearl barley, rinsed
- 6 cups chicken broth
- 1 bay leaf
- 1 teaspoon dried thyme
- Salt and pepper, to taste
- 1 cup pitted prunes
- Chopped fresh parsley, for garnish (optional)

Instructions:

1. Prepare the Chicken:
    - Place the whole chicken in a large pot and cover it with water. Bring to a boil over medium-high heat.
    - Reduce the heat to low and simmer the chicken, partially covered, for about 1 hour, or until the chicken is cooked through and tender.
    - Remove the chicken from the pot and let it cool slightly. Once cool enough to handle, remove the meat from the bones and shred or chop it into bite-sized pieces. Discard the skin and bones. Set the chicken meat aside.
2. Make the Soup:
    - In the same pot used to cook the chicken, heat a bit of oil over medium heat. Add the sliced leeks, diced carrots, diced celery, diced onion, and minced garlic. Cook, stirring occasionally, until the vegetables are softened, about 5-7 minutes.
    - Add the shredded chicken back to the pot along with the rinsed pearl barley, chicken broth, bay leaf, dried thyme, salt, and pepper.
    - Bring the soup to a simmer and cook, partially covered, for about 30-40 minutes, or until the barley is tender and cooked through.
3. Add the Prunes:

- Once the barley is cooked, stir in the pitted prunes. Simmer the soup for an additional 10 minutes to allow the flavors to meld together.
4. Serve:
    - Remove the bay leaf from the soup before serving.
    - Ladle the Cock-a-Leekie soup into bowls and garnish with chopped fresh parsley, if desired.
    - Serve the soup hot, accompanied by crusty bread for dipping.

Cock-a-Leekie soup is a comforting and nutritious dish that's perfect for warming up on cold days. The combination of chicken, leeks, barley, and prunes creates a rich and flavorful soup that's sure to satisfy. Enjoy this Scottish classic as a starter or as a light meal on its own.

Beef Stew and Dumplings

Ingredients:

For the beef stew:

- 2 lbs (about 900g) beef stew meat, cut into bite-sized pieces
- 2 tablespoons all-purpose flour
- Salt and pepper, to taste
- 2 tablespoons vegetable oil
- 1 onion, chopped
- 2 cloves garlic, minced
- 4 carrots, peeled and sliced
- 4 celery stalks, sliced
- 2 potatoes, peeled and diced
- 4 cups (960ml) beef broth
- 1 tablespoon Worcestershire sauce
- 2 bay leaves
- 1 teaspoon dried thyme
- 1 cup frozen peas (optional)
- Chopped fresh parsley, for garnish (optional)

For the dumplings:

- 1 cup (125g) all-purpose flour
- 2 teaspoons baking powder
- 1/2 teaspoon salt
- 2 tablespoons cold unsalted butter, cut into small cubes
- 1/2 cup (120ml) milk

Instructions:

1. Prepare the Beef Stew:
    - In a bowl, toss the beef stew meat with the all-purpose flour, salt, and pepper until evenly coated.
    - Heat the vegetable oil in a large pot or Dutch oven over medium-high heat. Add the coated beef stew meat and cook until browned on all sides, about 5-7 minutes. Remove the beef from the pot and set aside.

- In the same pot, add the chopped onion and minced garlic. Cook, stirring occasionally, until the onions are softened, about 3-4 minutes.
- Add the sliced carrots, celery, and diced potatoes to the pot. Cook for another 5 minutes, stirring occasionally.
- Return the browned beef to the pot. Pour in the beef broth, Worcestershire sauce, bay leaves, and dried thyme. Stir to combine.
- Bring the stew to a simmer, then reduce the heat to low. Cover and cook for 1.5 to 2 hours, or until the beef is tender and the vegetables are cooked through.
- If using frozen peas, add them to the stew during the last 10 minutes of cooking.
- Season the stew with additional salt and pepper to taste. Remove the bay leaves before serving.

2. Make the Dumplings:
    - In a mixing bowl, whisk together the all-purpose flour, baking powder, and salt.
    - Cut in the cold unsalted butter using a pastry cutter or fork until the mixture resembles coarse crumbs.
    - Gradually add the milk, stirring with a fork, until a soft dough forms.
    - Drop spoonfuls of the dumpling dough onto the surface of the simmering stew.
    - Cover the pot and let the dumplings cook for 15 minutes without lifting the lid. The dumplings will puff up and become fluffy.
3. Serve:
    - Once the dumplings are cooked through, remove the pot from the heat.
    - Ladle the beef stew and dumplings into bowls.
    - Garnish with chopped fresh parsley, if desired.
    - Serve hot and enjoy this comforting and hearty dish!

Beef stew and dumplings is a satisfying meal that's perfect for cozy dinners with family and friends. The tender beef, flavorful vegetables, and fluffy dumplings come together to create a delicious and comforting dish that's sure to warm you up from the inside out.

Mince and Tatties

Ingredients:

For the mince:

- 1 lb (450g) lean minced beef (ground beef)
- 1 onion, finely chopped
- 2 carrots, diced
- 2 cloves garlic, minced
- 2 tablespoons tomato paste
- 1 tablespoon Worcestershire sauce
- 2 cups (480ml) beef or vegetable broth
- 1 tablespoon vegetable oil
- Salt and pepper, to taste
- Chopped fresh parsley, for garnish (optional)

For the tatties:

- 2 lbs (about 900g) potatoes, peeled and cut into chunks
- 4 tablespoons unsalted butter
- 1/2 cup (120ml) milk or cream
- Salt and pepper, to taste

Instructions:

1. Prepare the Mince:
    - Heat the vegetable oil in a large skillet or saucepan over medium heat. Add the chopped onion and diced carrots. Cook until the vegetables are softened, about 5-7 minutes.
    - Add the minced garlic and cook for another minute until fragrant.
    - Add the minced beef to the skillet, breaking it up with a spoon, and cook until browned.
    - Stir in the tomato paste and Worcestershire sauce, and cook for another minute.

- Pour in the beef or vegetable broth, stirring to combine. Bring the mixture to a simmer.
- Reduce the heat to low and let the mince simmer gently for 20-30 minutes, stirring occasionally, until the sauce has thickened and the flavors have melded together.
- Season with salt and pepper to taste. Remove from heat and set aside.

2. Prepare the Tatties:
   - While the mince is simmering, place the potato chunks in a large pot of salted water. Bring to a boil and cook until the potatoes are fork-tender, about 15-20 minutes.
   - Drain the cooked potatoes and return them to the pot. Add the butter, milk or cream, salt, and pepper.
   - Mash the potatoes until smooth and creamy. Adjust seasoning to taste.

3. Serve:
   - To serve, spoon the mince onto serving plates or bowls.
   - Top the mince with a generous portion of mashed potatoes (tatties).
   - Garnish with chopped fresh parsley, if desired.
   - Serve hot and enjoy this comforting Scottish dish!

Mince and tatties is a hearty and satisfying meal that's perfect for a cozy dinner at home. It's a classic comfort food dish that's sure to warm you up on chilly evenings. Feel free to customize the recipe with your favorite herbs and spices for extra flavor!

Chicken and Mushroom Pie

Ingredients:

For the filling:

- 2 tablespoons unsalted butter
- 1 onion, finely chopped
- 2 cloves garlic, minced
- 1 lb (450g) boneless, skinless chicken breasts or thighs, cut into bite-sized pieces
- 8 oz (225g) mushrooms, sliced
- 1/4 cup (30g) all-purpose flour
- 1 cup (240ml) chicken broth
- 1 cup (240ml) milk or cream
- 1 teaspoon dried thyme
- Salt and pepper, to taste
- 1/2 cup frozen peas (optional)
- Chopped fresh parsley, for garnish (optional)

For the pastry:

- 1 sheet of puff pastry, thawed if frozen
- 1 egg, beaten (for egg wash)

Instructions:

1. Prepare the Filling:
    - In a large skillet or saucepan, melt the butter over medium heat. Add the chopped onion and minced garlic, and cook until softened, about 3-4 minutes.
    - Add the chicken pieces to the skillet and cook until browned on all sides, about 5-7 minutes.
    - Add the sliced mushrooms to the skillet and cook until they release their juices and become tender, about 5 minutes.
    - Sprinkle the flour over the chicken and mushroom mixture, stirring to coat evenly.

- Gradually pour in the chicken broth and milk or cream, stirring constantly to prevent lumps from forming.
- Stir in the dried thyme, salt, and pepper to taste. Bring the mixture to a simmer and cook for 5-7 minutes, or until the sauce has thickened.
- If using frozen peas, stir them into the filling mixture. Cook for an additional 2-3 minutes until heated through. Remove from heat and let cool slightly.

2. Assemble the Pie:
   - Preheat your oven to 400°F (200°C).
   - Transfer the chicken and mushroom filling to a pie dish or individual ramekins, spreading it out evenly.

3. Prepare the Pastry:
   - Roll out the puff pastry sheet on a lightly floured surface to fit the top of the pie dish or ramekins. Cut the pastry to size, leaving a slight overhang.
   - Brush the edges of the pie dish or ramekins with beaten egg.
   - Place the pastry over the filling, pressing down gently around the edges to seal. Trim any excess pastry and crimp the edges with a fork to create a decorative border.
   - Use a sharp knife to make a few small slits in the center of the pastry to allow steam to escape.

4. Bake the Pie:
   - Place the assembled pie on a baking sheet and brush the top of the pastry with beaten egg for a golden finish.
   - Bake in the preheated oven for 25-30 minutes, or until the pastry is puffed and golden brown.

5. Serve:
   - Remove the chicken and mushroom pie from the oven and let it cool for a few minutes before serving.
   - Garnish with chopped fresh parsley, if desired.
   - Serve the pie hot, with your favorite side dishes such as mashed potatoes and steamed vegetables.

Chicken and mushroom pie is a comforting and satisfying meal that's perfect for dinner any day of the week. Enjoy the combination of tender chicken, earthy mushrooms, and creamy sauce encased in buttery, flaky pastry!

Apple Crumble

Ingredients:

For the apple filling:

- 6 medium-sized apples (such as Granny Smith or Braeburn), peeled, cored, and sliced
- 1/4 cup (50g) granulated sugar
- 1 tablespoon lemon juice
- 1 teaspoon ground cinnamon
- 1/4 teaspoon ground nutmeg
- 1 tablespoon all-purpose flour

For the crumble topping:

- 1 cup (120g) all-purpose flour
- 1/2 cup (100g) granulated sugar
- 1/2 cup (110g) unsalted butter, chilled and cut into small cubes
- 1/2 cup (45g) old-fashioned rolled oats
- 1/4 teaspoon salt

Instructions:

1. Preheat the Oven:
    - Preheat your oven to 375°F (190°C). Lightly grease a 9x9-inch (23x23cm) baking dish or a similar-sized ovenproof dish.
2. Prepare the Apple Filling:
    - In a large mixing bowl, combine the sliced apples, granulated sugar, lemon juice, ground cinnamon, ground nutmeg, and all-purpose flour. Toss until the apples are evenly coated with the sugar and spices.
    - Transfer the apple mixture to the prepared baking dish, spreading it out evenly.
3. Make the Crumble Topping:
    - In a separate mixing bowl, combine the all-purpose flour, granulated sugar, chilled butter cubes, rolled oats, and salt.
    - Use your fingertips or a pastry cutter to rub the butter into the flour mixture until it resembles coarse crumbs and the butter is evenly distributed.

4. Assemble and Bake:
   - Sprinkle the crumble topping evenly over the apple filling in the baking dish.
   - Place the baking dish on a baking sheet to catch any drips during baking.
   - Bake in the preheated oven for 35-40 minutes, or until the apple filling is bubbling and the crumble topping is golden brown and crispy.
5. Serve:
   - Remove the apple crumble from the oven and let it cool for a few minutes before serving.
   - Serve warm, with a scoop of vanilla ice cream or a dollop of whipped cream, if desired.

Apple crumble is best enjoyed fresh out of the oven when the topping is crunchy and the apple filling is warm and bubbly. It's a comforting and nostalgic dessert that's perfect for any occasion, from casual family dinners to holiday gatherings. Enjoy the delicious combination of sweet, spiced apples and buttery crumble topping!

Bread and Butter Pudding

Ingredients:

- 8 slices of day-old bread (white or wholemeal), crusts removed
- Butter, softened, for spreading
- 1/3 cup (75g) raisins or sultanas (optional)
- 4 large eggs
- 1/2 cup (100g) granulated sugar, plus extra for sprinkling
- 2 cups (480ml) milk or cream
- 1 teaspoon vanilla extract
- Ground cinnamon, for sprinkling
- Ground nutmeg, for sprinkling
- Whipped cream or custard, for serving (optional)

Instructions:

1. Prepare the Bread:
    - Preheat your oven to 350°F (180°C). Lightly grease a baking dish with butter.
    - Spread butter on one side of each slice of bread. Arrange half of the bread slices, buttered-side up, in the prepared baking dish. If using, sprinkle half of the raisins or sultanas over the bread.
2. Prepare the Custard Mixture:
    - In a mixing bowl, whisk together the eggs and granulated sugar until well combined.
    - Gradually whisk in the milk or cream and vanilla extract until smooth and creamy.
3. Assemble the Pudding:
    - Pour half of the custard mixture evenly over the bread slices in the baking dish. Allow the bread to soak up the custard for a few minutes.
    - Arrange the remaining bread slices on top, buttered-side up. If using, sprinkle the remaining raisins or sultanas over the bread.
    - Pour the remaining custard mixture evenly over the top layer of bread slices, ensuring that all the bread is soaked in the custard.
4. Bake the Pudding:
    - Sprinkle the top of the pudding with a little extra granulated sugar, ground cinnamon, and ground nutmeg for added flavor.

- Place the baking dish in the preheated oven and bake for 30-35 minutes, or until the pudding is golden brown and set, and the custard is cooked through.
5. Serve:
    - Remove the bread and butter pudding from the oven and let it cool for a few minutes before serving.
    - Serve warm, optionally topped with whipped cream or custard.
    - Enjoy this comforting and nostalgic dessert!

Bread and butter pudding is a simple yet delicious dessert that's perfect for using up leftover bread. It's wonderfully custardy and aromatic, with a hint of sweetness from the raisins and warmth from the spices. Serve it as a comforting treat for dessert or even as a special breakfast dish.

Cheese and Onion Pie

Ingredients:

For the pastry:

- 2 cups (250g) all-purpose flour
- 1/2 teaspoon salt
- 1/2 cup (115g) unsalted butter, cold and cubed
- 4-6 tablespoons cold water

For the filling:

- 2 large onions, thinly sliced
- 2 tablespoons unsalted butter
- 2 tablespoons all-purpose flour
- 1 cup (240ml) milk
- 2 cups (200g) grated cheese (such as cheddar or Gruyere)
- Salt and pepper, to taste
- 1 egg, beaten (for egg wash)

Instructions:

1. Prepare the Pastry:
   - In a large mixing bowl, combine the all-purpose flour and salt. Add the cold, cubed butter to the flour mixture.
   - Use your fingertips or a pastry cutter to rub the butter into the flour until the mixture resembles coarse crumbs.
   - Gradually add the cold water, one tablespoon at a time, stirring with a fork, until the dough comes together.
   - Shape the dough into a ball, wrap it in plastic wrap, and refrigerate for at least 30 minutes.
2. Make the Filling:
   - In a large skillet, melt the butter over medium heat. Add the thinly sliced onions and cook, stirring occasionally, until softened and caramelized, about 15-20 minutes.

- Sprinkle the cooked onions with the all-purpose flour and stir to coat evenly. Cook for another minute.
- Gradually pour in the milk, stirring constantly, until the mixture thickens and becomes smooth.
- Stir in the grated cheese until melted and well combined. Season with salt and pepper to taste. Remove from heat and let the filling cool slightly.

3. Assemble the Pie:
   - Preheat your oven to 375°F (190°C). Lightly grease a pie dish or tart pan.
   - Roll out the chilled pastry dough on a lightly floured surface to fit the size of your pie dish. Line the pie dish with the pastry dough, trimming any excess.
   - Pour the cheese and onion filling into the pastry-lined dish, spreading it out evenly.

4. Top the Pie:
   - Roll out the remaining pastry dough to create a top crust for the pie. You can either cover the pie completely or create a lattice pattern for the top crust.
   - Trim any excess dough and crimp the edges to seal. Use a sharp knife to make a few small slits in the center of the pie to allow steam to escape.
   - Brush the top of the pie with beaten egg for a golden finish.

5. Bake the Pie:
   - Place the assembled pie on a baking sheet to catch any drips during baking.
   - Bake in the preheated oven for 30-35 minutes, or until the pastry is golden brown and the filling is bubbling.

6. Serve:
   - Remove the cheese and onion pie from the oven and let it cool for a few minutes before serving.
   - Slice and serve warm, accompanied by a side salad or your favorite vegetables.

Cheese and onion pie is a delicious and satisfying dish that's perfect for lunch or dinner. Enjoy the creamy cheese filling, studded with caramelized onions, encased in buttery pastry crust.

Corned Beef Hash

Ingredients:

- 2 cups cooked corned beef, diced
- 2 cups potatoes, peeled and diced into small cubes
- 1 onion, diced
- 2 tablespoons butter or vegetable oil
- Salt and pepper to taste
- Optional: chopped fresh parsley or green onions for garnish

Instructions:

1. If you haven't already, cook the corned beef. You can use leftover corned beef from a previous meal or cook it specifically for this dish. You can boil it, roast it, or use a slow cooker. Once cooked, dice the corned beef into small cubes.
2. In a large skillet, melt the butter over medium heat. You can also use vegetable oil if you prefer.
3. Add the diced onion to the skillet and cook until softened and translucent, about 3-5 minutes.
4. Add the diced potatoes to the skillet. Spread them out evenly and let them cook without stirring for a few minutes to allow them to brown on one side. Then, stir occasionally to ensure even cooking.
5. Once the potatoes are cooked through and starting to brown, add the diced corned beef to the skillet. Stir to combine with the potatoes and onions.
6. Cook the mixture for another 5-7 minutes, stirring occasionally, until everything is heated through and the hash is crispy and golden brown.
7. Season with salt and pepper to taste. You can also add any additional herbs or spices you like at this point, such as thyme or paprika.
8. Once done, transfer the corned beef hash to serving plates and garnish with chopped fresh parsley or green onions if desired.
9. Serve hot and enjoy your homemade corned beef hash for breakfast, brunch, or any meal of the day!

Feel free to customize this recipe to your liking by adding other ingredients like bell peppers, garlic, or even cheese. Enjoy!

Chicken Balti

Ingredients:

- 500g boneless, skinless chicken thighs or breasts, cut into bite-sized pieces
- 2 tablespoons vegetable oil
- 2 onions, finely chopped
- 3 garlic cloves, minced
- 1-inch piece of ginger, grated
- 2 green chilies, finely chopped (adjust to taste)
- 2 teaspoons ground coriander
- 2 teaspoons ground cumin
- 1 teaspoon ground turmeric
- 1 teaspoon paprika
- 1 teaspoon garam masala
- 1 teaspoon ground fenugreek (optional)
- 400g canned chopped tomatoes
- 1 green bell pepper, diced
- 1 red bell pepper, diced
- 2 tablespoons tomato paste
- Salt to taste
- Fresh coriander leaves (cilantro) for garnish
- Lemon wedges for serving

For the Balti Paste:

- 2 tablespoons vegetable oil
- 2 onions, roughly chopped
- 3 garlic cloves
- 1-inch piece of ginger
- 2 tomatoes, roughly chopped
- 2 green chilies, chopped
- 1 tablespoon ground coriander
- 1 tablespoon ground cumin
- 1 teaspoon ground turmeric
- 1 teaspoon paprika
- 1 teaspoon garam masala

Instructions:

1. Start by making the Balti paste. In a blender or food processor, combine all the ingredients for the Balti paste and blend until smooth. Set aside.
2. Heat 2 tablespoons of vegetable oil in a large, heavy-bottomed pan or Balti dish over medium heat. Add the chopped onions and cook until softened and translucent, about 5-7 minutes.
3. Add the minced garlic, grated ginger, and chopped green chilies to the pan. Cook for another 2 minutes, stirring frequently.
4. Add the Balti paste to the pan and cook for 3-4 minutes, stirring constantly to prevent sticking.
5. Add the ground coriander, cumin, turmeric, paprika, garam masala, and ground fenugreek (if using) to the pan. Stir well to combine with the paste and cook for another 2 minutes.
6. Add the diced chicken pieces to the pan and cook until they are sealed and starting to brown, about 5 minutes.
7. Stir in the canned chopped tomatoes, tomato paste, diced green bell pepper, and diced red bell pepper. Season with salt to taste.
8. Reduce the heat to low, cover the pan, and simmer gently for 20-25 minutes, or until the chicken is cooked through and the sauce has thickened.
9. Once done, garnish with fresh coriander leaves (cilantro) and serve hot with naan bread, rice, or roti. Serve with lemon wedges on the side for squeezing over the curry for extra flavor.

Enjoy your homemade Chicken Balti! Adjust the spiciness according to your preference by adding more or fewer green chilies.

Gammon Steak with Pineapple

Ingredients:

- 2 gammon steaks (about 200-250g each)
- 4 pineapple slices (fresh or canned)
- 2 tablespoons vegetable oil
- Salt and pepper to taste
- 2 tablespoons brown sugar (optional)
- Fresh parsley for garnish (optional)

Instructions:

1. If using fresh pineapple, peel and core the pineapple, then slice it into rings. If using canned pineapple, drain the slices.
2. Preheat your grill or grill pan to medium-high heat.
3. Brush the gammon steaks with vegetable oil on both sides and season with salt and pepper.
4. Place the gammon steaks on the preheated grill or grill pan. Cook for about 4-5 minutes on each side, or until they are cooked through and have nice grill marks. Cooking time may vary depending on the thickness of the steaks.
5. While the gammon steaks are cooking, you can grill the pineapple slices alongside them. Place the pineapple slices on the grill and cook for about 2-3 minutes on each side, or until they have grill marks and are slightly caramelized. If you like, you can sprinkle a little brown sugar over the pineapple slices before grilling for extra caramelization.
6. Once the gammon steaks and pineapple slices are cooked, remove them from the grill and transfer to serving plates.
7. Serve the gammon steaks topped with grilled pineapple slices. You can garnish with fresh parsley if desired.
8. Enjoy your gammon steak with pineapple alongside your favorite side dishes, such as mashed potatoes, steamed vegetables, or a fresh salad.

This dish is simple yet flavorful, making it perfect for a quick and satisfying meal. Adjust the seasoning and grilling time according to your taste preferences.

Lamb Shank

Ingredients:

- 4 lamb shanks
- Salt and black pepper to taste
- 2 tablespoons olive oil
- 1 onion, chopped
- 2 carrots, chopped
- 2 celery stalks, chopped
- 4 garlic cloves, minced
- 2 cups beef or vegetable broth
- 1 cup red wine (optional)
- 2 bay leaves
- 2 sprigs fresh rosemary
- 2 sprigs fresh thyme
- 2 tablespoons tomato paste
- 2 tablespoons Worcestershire sauce
- 1 tablespoon balsamic vinegar
- 1 tablespoon honey (optional)
- Chopped fresh parsley for garnish

Instructions:

1. Preheat your oven to 325°F (160°C).
2. Season the lamb shanks generously with salt and black pepper.
3. Heat the olive oil in a large oven-safe pot or Dutch oven over medium-high heat. Add the lamb shanks and sear them on all sides until browned, about 4-5 minutes per side. Remove the lamb shanks from the pot and set aside.
4. In the same pot, add the chopped onion, carrots, and celery. Cook, stirring occasionally, until the vegetables are softened, about 5 minutes.
5. Add the minced garlic to the pot and cook for another minute, until fragrant.
6. Pour in the beef or vegetable broth and red wine (if using), scraping up any browned bits from the bottom of the pot.
7. Add the bay leaves, rosemary, and thyme sprigs to the pot. Stir in the tomato paste, Worcestershire sauce, balsamic vinegar, and honey (if using).
8. Return the lamb shanks to the pot, nestling them into the liquid and vegetables.

9. Cover the pot with a lid and transfer it to the preheated oven. Braise the lamb shanks for 2.5 to 3 hours, or until the meat is tender and falling off the bone.
10. Once the lamb shanks are done, remove them from the pot and keep warm.
11. If desired, you can strain the braising liquid to remove the vegetables and herbs, then return the liquid to the pot and simmer until it thickens slightly to make a sauce. Alternatively, you can serve the lamb shanks with the vegetables and herbs as they are.
12. Serve the lamb shanks hot, drizzled with the sauce and garnished with chopped fresh parsley.

Braised lamb shanks pair beautifully with mashed potatoes, creamy polenta, or crusty bread to soak up the delicious sauce. Enjoy!

Prawn Cocktail

Ingredients:

For the Cocktail Sauce:

- 1/2 cup mayonnaise
- 2 tablespoons ketchup
- 1 tablespoon lemon juice
- 1 teaspoon Worcestershire sauce
- 1/2 teaspoon hot sauce (such as Tabasco), or to taste
- Salt and pepper to taste

For the Prawn Cocktail:

- 500g large prawns (shrimp), cooked and peeled
- 2-3 cups shredded lettuce (such as iceberg or romaine)
- Lemon wedges, for garnish
- Fresh parsley, chopped, for garnish

Instructions:

1. In a small bowl, whisk together all the ingredients for the cocktail sauce until well combined. Taste and adjust the seasoning, adding more lemon juice, Worcestershire sauce, hot sauce, salt, or pepper as needed. Cover the sauce and refrigerate until ready to use.
2. If the prawns are not already cooked and peeled, prepare them according to the package instructions. Once cooked and peeled, let them cool to room temperature or chill them in the refrigerator until ready to use.
3. When ready to serve, divide the shredded lettuce among serving glasses or small bowls, creating a bed for the prawns.
4. Arrange the cooked prawns on top of the shredded lettuce in each glass or bowl.
5. Spoon the cocktail sauce over the prawns, covering them generously.
6. Garnish each serving with a lemon wedge and a sprinkle of chopped fresh parsley.
7. Serve the prawn cocktail immediately as an appetizer or starter.

Enjoy your homemade prawn cocktail! It's a refreshing and flavorful dish that's perfect for entertaining or as a special treat for yourself. Feel free to customize the cocktail sauce to your taste preferences by adjusting the levels of tanginess, spiciness, or sweetness.

Beef Bourguignon

Ingredients:

- 1.5 kg (3.3 lbs) beef chuck or stewing beef, cut into chunks
- Salt and pepper to taste
- 2 tablespoons olive oil
- 200g (7 oz) bacon or pancetta, diced
- 2 onions, chopped
- 3 carrots, chopped
- 3 cloves garlic, minced
- 2 tablespoons all-purpose flour
- 750ml (3 cups) red wine (Burgundy or another dry red wine)
- 500ml (2 cups) beef broth
- 2 tablespoons tomato paste
- 2 bay leaves
- 2 sprigs fresh thyme
- 250g (about 9 oz) pearl onions, peeled
- 250g (about 9 oz) button mushrooms, halved or quartered if large
- Chopped fresh parsley for garnish (optional)

Instructions:

1. Preheat your oven to 160°C (320°F).
2. Pat the beef chunks dry with paper towels and season generously with salt and pepper.
3. Heat the olive oil in a large oven-safe pot or Dutch oven over medium-high heat. Add the diced bacon or pancetta and cook until crispy. Remove the bacon with a slotted spoon and set aside, leaving the rendered fat in the pot.
4. In the same pot, add the beef chunks in batches, making sure not to overcrowd the pot. Brown the beef on all sides, then transfer to a plate and set aside.
5. Add the chopped onions and carrots to the pot. Cook, stirring occasionally, until the vegetables are softened, about 5 minutes.
6. Add the minced garlic and cook for another minute, until fragrant.
7. Sprinkle the flour over the vegetables in the pot and stir to coat evenly.
8. Return the beef and bacon to the pot. Pour in the red wine and beef broth, stirring to deglaze the pot and scrape up any browned bits from the bottom.

9. Stir in the tomato paste, bay leaves, and thyme sprigs.
10. Cover the pot with a lid and transfer it to the preheated oven. Cook for about 2.5 to 3 hours, or until the beef is tender and the sauce has thickened.
11. About 30 minutes before the Beef Bourguignon is done, add the pearl onions and mushrooms to the pot. Stir to combine and continue cooking until the vegetables are tender.
12. Once done, remove the pot from the oven and discard the bay leaves and thyme sprigs. Taste and adjust the seasoning with salt and pepper if needed.
13. Serve the Beef Bourguignon hot, garnished with chopped fresh parsley if desired. It pairs well with crusty bread, mashed potatoes, or buttered noodles.

Enjoy your homemade Beef Bourguignon, a comforting and satisfying French classic!

Rabbit Stew

Ingredients:

- 1 whole rabbit, cut into serving pieces
- Salt and pepper to taste
- 2 tablespoons olive oil or vegetable oil
- 1 onion, chopped
- 2 carrots, chopped
- 2 celery stalks, chopped
- 3 cloves garlic, minced
- 2 tablespoons all-purpose flour
- 2 cups chicken or vegetable broth
- 1 cup dry white wine (optional)
- 2 bay leaves
- 2 sprigs fresh thyme
- 2 potatoes, peeled and diced
- 2 cups diced tomatoes (canned or fresh)
- Chopped fresh parsley for garnish (optional)

Instructions:

1. Season the rabbit pieces with salt and pepper.
2. Heat the olive oil in a large pot or Dutch oven over medium-high heat. Add the rabbit pieces in batches and brown them on all sides. Remove the browned rabbit pieces from the pot and set aside.
3. In the same pot, add the chopped onion, carrots, and celery. Cook, stirring occasionally, until the vegetables are softened, about 5 minutes.
4. Add the minced garlic to the pot and cook for another minute, until fragrant.
5. Sprinkle the flour over the vegetables in the pot and stir to coat evenly.
6. Return the browned rabbit pieces to the pot. Pour in the chicken or vegetable broth and white wine (if using), stirring to combine.
7. Add the bay leaves and thyme sprigs to the pot.
8. Cover the pot with a lid and simmer the stew over low heat for about 1.5 to 2 hours, or until the rabbit is tender.
9. Add the diced potatoes and diced tomatoes to the pot. Stir to combine.

10. Continue simmering the stew, uncovered, for another 30 minutes to 1 hour, or until the potatoes are cooked through and the stew has thickened to your desired consistency.
11. Once done, discard the bay leaves and thyme sprigs. Taste and adjust the seasoning with salt and pepper if needed.
12. Serve the rabbit stew hot, garnished with chopped fresh parsley if desired. It pairs well with crusty bread, rice, or mashed potatoes.

Enjoy your homemade rabbit stew, a comforting and flavorful dish that's sure to satisfy!

Liver and Onions

Ingredients:

- 500g (1 lb) beef liver, sliced
- Salt and pepper to taste
- All-purpose flour, for dredging
- 2 tablespoons vegetable oil or butter
- 2 large onions, thinly sliced
- 2 cloves garlic, minced (optional)
- 1/2 cup beef broth or water
- 1 tablespoon Worcestershire sauce (optional)
- Chopped fresh parsley for garnish (optional)

Instructions:

1. Start by rinsing the liver slices under cold water and patting them dry with paper towels. Season the liver slices with salt and pepper on both sides.
2. Dredge the liver slices in flour, shaking off any excess.
3. Heat the vegetable oil or butter in a large skillet over medium-high heat. Once hot, add the liver slices to the skillet in a single layer, making sure not to overcrowd the pan. Cook the liver slices for about 2-3 minutes on each side, or until they are browned and cooked through. Cooking time may vary depending on the thickness of the liver slices. Remove the cooked liver slices from the skillet and set aside.
4. In the same skillet, add the sliced onions and minced garlic (if using). Cook, stirring occasionally, until the onions are soft and golden brown, about 8-10 minutes.
5. Once the onions are caramelized, pour in the beef broth or water and Worcestershire sauce (if using). Stir to deglaze the pan, scraping up any browned bits from the bottom.
6. Return the cooked liver slices to the skillet, nestling them among the onions. Reduce the heat to low and simmer the liver and onions together for another 5 minutes, allowing the flavors to meld.
7. Taste the liver and onions and adjust the seasoning with salt and pepper if needed.

8. Once done, transfer the liver and onions to serving plates. Garnish with chopped fresh parsley if desired.
9. Serve the liver and onions hot, accompanied by mashed potatoes, rice, or crusty bread.

Enjoy your homemade liver and onions, a comforting and satisfying dish that's perfect for a cozy meal at home!

Chicken Liver Pâté

Ingredients:

- 400g (14 oz) chicken livers, trimmed
- 1 onion, finely chopped
- 2 cloves garlic, minced
- 4 tablespoons butter
- 2 tablespoons olive oil
- 2 tablespoons brandy or cognac (optional)
- 1 teaspoon fresh thyme leaves (or 1/2 teaspoon dried thyme)
- Salt and pepper to taste
- 1/4 cup heavy cream
- Toasted bread slices or crackers, for serving

Instructions:

1. Rinse the chicken livers under cold water and pat them dry with paper towels. Trim any excess fat or connective tissue.
2. Heat 2 tablespoons of butter and 1 tablespoon of olive oil in a large skillet over medium heat. Add the chopped onion and minced garlic, and cook until softened and translucent, about 5 minutes.
3. Increase the heat to medium-high and add the chicken livers to the skillet. Cook the livers until they are browned on the outside but still slightly pink on the inside, about 3-4 minutes per side.
4. Remove the skillet from the heat and let the livers cool slightly.
5. Transfer the cooked chicken livers, onions, and garlic to a food processor. Add the remaining 2 tablespoons of butter, 1 tablespoon of olive oil, brandy or cognac (if using), fresh thyme leaves, salt, and pepper.
6. Pulse the mixture in the food processor until smooth and creamy. Scrape down the sides of the bowl as needed to ensure everything is evenly blended.
7. With the food processor running, gradually pour in the heavy cream until the pâté reaches your desired consistency. You may need to add more or less cream depending on how creamy you like it.
8. Taste the pâté and adjust the seasoning with salt and pepper if needed.
9. Transfer the pâté to a serving dish or ramekins. Smooth the top with a spatula and cover with plastic wrap, pressing it directly onto the surface of the pâté to prevent it from forming a skin.

10. Refrigerate the pâté for at least 1-2 hours to allow it to firm up and develop flavor.
11. Serve the chicken liver pâté chilled or at room temperature, accompanied by toasted bread slices or crackers.

Enjoy your homemade chicken liver pâté, a delicious and elegant spread that's sure to impress!

Mushy Peas

Ingredients:

- 500g (about 2 cups) frozen peas
- 2 tablespoons butter
- 1 small onion, finely chopped
- 1 clove garlic, minced (optional)
- Salt and pepper to taste
- 1/2 cup vegetable or chicken broth
- 2 tablespoons heavy cream or milk (optional)

Instructions:

1. Cook the frozen peas according to the package instructions. Drain and set aside.
2. In a large skillet or saucepan, melt the butter over medium heat.
3. Add the chopped onion to the skillet and cook until softened and translucent, about 5 minutes. If using garlic, add it to the skillet and cook for another minute until fragrant.
4. Add the cooked peas to the skillet and stir to combine with the onions and garlic.
5. Using a potato masher or fork, mash the peas to your desired consistency. Some people prefer completely smooth mushy peas, while others like them slightly chunky. Mash them until they reach your preferred texture.
6. Season the mushy peas with salt and pepper to taste.
7. Pour in the vegetable or chicken broth, stirring to combine. This will help loosen the peas and create a creamy texture.
8. If desired, stir in the heavy cream or milk to add extra richness to the mushy peas.
9. Cook the mushy peas for another 2-3 minutes, or until heated through and creamy.
10. Taste and adjust the seasoning if needed.
11. Serve the mushy peas hot as a side dish or topping for your favorite British meals, such as fish and chips or meat pies.

Enjoy your homemade mushy peas, a classic and comforting side dish that pairs perfectly with a variety of dishes!

Pea and Ham Soup

Ingredients:

- 1 tablespoon olive oil
- 1 onion, chopped
- 2 carrots, chopped
- 2 celery stalks, chopped
- 2 cloves garlic, minced
- 200g (about 1 cup) dried split peas, rinsed and drained
- 200g (about 1 cup) diced cooked ham
- 6 cups chicken or vegetable broth
- 1 bay leaf
- 1 teaspoon dried thyme
- Salt and pepper to taste
- Chopped fresh parsley for garnish (optional)

Instructions:

1. Heat the olive oil in a large pot or Dutch oven over medium heat. Add the chopped onion, carrots, and celery. Cook, stirring occasionally, until the vegetables are softened, about 5-7 minutes.
2. Add the minced garlic to the pot and cook for another minute, until fragrant.
3. Stir in the dried split peas and diced cooked ham, coating them with the vegetables.
4. Pour in the chicken or vegetable broth, stirring to combine. Add the bay leaf and dried thyme to the pot.
5. Bring the soup to a boil, then reduce the heat to low. Cover the pot and simmer the soup for about 1 to 1.5 hours, or until the peas are tender and the soup has thickened, stirring occasionally.
6. Once the soup is cooked and the peas are tender, remove the bay leaf from the pot. Taste the soup and season with salt and pepper as needed.
7. If you prefer a smoother texture, you can use an immersion blender to partially blend the soup until it reaches your desired consistency. Alternatively, you can leave the soup chunky.
8. Serve the pea and ham soup hot, garnished with chopped fresh parsley if desired.

9. Enjoy your homemade pea and ham soup as a comforting meal on its own or with crusty bread on the side.

This soup also freezes well, so you can make a big batch and store leftovers for later.

Just be sure to cool it completely before transferring to airtight containers for freezing.

Leek and Potato Soup

Ingredients:

- 2 tablespoons butter or olive oil
- 3 leeks, white and light green parts only, sliced
- 2 cloves garlic, minced
- 3 medium potatoes, peeled and diced
- 4 cups vegetable or chicken broth
- Salt and pepper to taste
- 1/2 cup heavy cream or milk (optional)
- Chopped fresh chives or parsley for garnish (optional)

Instructions:

1. In a large pot or Dutch oven, melt the butter or heat the olive oil over medium heat.
2. Add the sliced leeks to the pot and cook, stirring occasionally, until they are softened, about 5-7 minutes.
3. Add the minced garlic to the pot and cook for another minute, until fragrant.
4. Stir in the diced potatoes and cook for a few minutes, allowing them to lightly brown.
5. Pour in the vegetable or chicken broth, stirring to combine. Bring the mixture to a simmer.
6. Cover the pot and let the soup simmer for about 15-20 minutes, or until the potatoes are tender when pierced with a fork.
7. Once the potatoes are cooked, use an immersion blender to blend the soup until smooth. Alternatively, you can transfer the soup in batches to a blender and blend until smooth, then return it to the pot.
8. If using, stir in the heavy cream or milk to add richness to the soup. Season with salt and pepper to taste.
9. Continue to cook the soup for another few minutes, allowing the flavors to meld.
10. Serve the leek and potato soup hot, garnished with chopped fresh chives or parsley if desired.
11. Enjoy your homemade leek and potato soup as a comforting meal on its own or with crusty bread on the side.

This soup can be easily customized by adding additional vegetables or herbs to suit your taste preferences. It's also a great way to use up leftover potatoes and leeks!

Stilton and Broccoli Soup

Ingredients:

- 2 tablespoons butter
- 1 onion, chopped
- 2 cloves garlic, minced
- 3 cups broccoli florets
- 4 cups vegetable or chicken broth
- Salt and pepper to taste
- 1 cup milk or heavy cream
- 150g Stilton cheese, crumbled (or another blue cheese of your choice)
- Chopped fresh chives or parsley for garnish (optional)

Instructions:

1. In a large pot or Dutch oven, melt the butter over medium heat.
2. Add the chopped onion to the pot and cook, stirring occasionally, until softened, about 5 minutes.
3. Add the minced garlic to the pot and cook for another minute, until fragrant.
4. Add the broccoli florets to the pot and stir to combine with the onions and garlic.
5. Pour in the vegetable or chicken broth, stirring to combine. Bring the mixture to a simmer.
6. Cover the pot and let the soup simmer for about 15-20 minutes, or until the broccoli is tender when pierced with a fork.
7. Once the broccoli is cooked, use an immersion blender to blend the soup until smooth. Alternatively, you can transfer the soup in batches to a blender and blend until smooth, then return it to the pot.
8. Stir in the milk or heavy cream to add richness to the soup. Season with salt and pepper to taste.
9. Add the crumbled Stilton cheese to the pot and stir until the cheese is melted and incorporated into the soup.
10. Continue to cook the soup for another few minutes, allowing the flavors to meld.
11. Serve the Stilton and broccoli soup hot, garnished with chopped fresh chives or parsley if desired.
12. Enjoy your homemade Stilton and broccoli soup as a comforting and flavorful meal on its own or with crusty bread on the side.

Feel free to adjust the amount of Stilton cheese according to your taste preferences.

You can also customize the soup by adding additional vegetables or herbs if desired.

Salmon en Croute

Ingredients:

- 2 salmon fillets (about 200g each), skin removed
- Salt and pepper to taste
- 1 sheet puff pastry, thawed if frozen
- 2 tablespoons Dijon mustard
- 100g spinach leaves, washed and dried
- 100g cream cheese, softened
- 1 egg, beaten (for egg wash)
- Sesame seeds or poppy seeds for garnish (optional)
- Lemon wedges for serving

Instructions:

1. Preheat your oven to 200°C (400°F) and line a baking sheet with parchment paper.
2. Season the salmon fillets with salt and pepper to taste.
3. On a lightly floured surface, roll out the puff pastry sheet to a size large enough to wrap around the salmon fillets.
4. Spread a thin layer of Dijon mustard over each salmon fillet.
5. Place a layer of spinach leaves on top of the mustard-coated salmon fillets.
6. Spread the softened cream cheese over the spinach leaves.
7. Place one salmon fillet, mustard side down, on one end of the puff pastry sheet. Place the other fillet, mustard side down, on the other end of the pastry sheet.
8. Fold the puff pastry over the salmon fillets, sealing the edges and ends by pressing them together. Trim any excess pastry if necessary.
9. Place the salmon en croute seam side down on the prepared baking sheet.
10. Brush the beaten egg over the top and sides of the pastry to create a shiny glaze.
11. If desired, sprinkle sesame seeds or poppy seeds over the top of the pastry for added texture and flavor.
12. Using a sharp knife, make a few small slits in the pastry to allow steam to escape during baking.
13. Bake the salmon en croute in the preheated oven for 20-25 minutes, or until the pastry is golden brown and crisp, and the salmon is cooked through.

14. Once done, remove the salmon en croute from the oven and let it rest for a few minutes before slicing.
15. Serve the salmon en croute hot, accompanied by lemon wedges for squeezing over the top.

Enjoy your homemade salmon en croute, a sophisticated and delicious dish that's sure to impress!

Haggis, Neeps, and Tatties

Haggis:

- 1 haggis (store-bought or homemade)
- 1 onion, finely chopped (optional)
- 2 tablespoons butter (optional)

Neeps (Turnips or Swedes):

- 2 large turnips or swedes
- 2 tablespoons butter
- Salt and pepper to taste

Tatties (Potatoes):

- 4 large potatoes, peeled and chopped into chunks
- 2 tablespoons butter
- Salt and pepper to taste

Instructions:

1. Cook the haggis according to the package instructions. If using a whole haggis, remove it from its casing and break it up with a fork.
2. If desired, sauté the chopped onion in butter until softened, then mix it into the cooked haggis for added flavor.
3. For the neeps, peel the turnips or swedes and chop them into chunks. Boil them in a large pot of salted water until tender, about 20-25 minutes. Drain well.
4. Mash the cooked turnips or swedes with butter until smooth. Season with salt and pepper to taste.
5. For the tatties, boil the potatoes in a large pot of salted water until tender, about 15-20 minutes. Drain well.
6. Mash the cooked potatoes with butter until smooth. Season with salt and pepper to taste.

7. To serve, plate a portion of haggis, neeps, and tatties on each plate. Traditionally, the haggis is placed in the center, surrounded by neeps on one side and tatties on the other.
8. Enjoy your haggis, neeps, and tatties with a dram of whisky and maybe even a reading of Robert Burns' poetry to complete the Burns Night celebration!

This dish is hearty, flavorful, and a true taste of Scottish tradition. Adjust the seasonings and proportions to suit your taste preferences.

Beef and Guinness Stew

Ingredients:

- 1.5 kg (3.3 lbs) beef chuck or stewing beef, cut into bite-sized pieces
- Salt and pepper to taste
- 2 tablespoons olive oil
- 2 onions, chopped
- 3 carrots, chopped
- 3 celery stalks, chopped
- 3 cloves garlic, minced
- 2 tablespoons all-purpose flour
- 500ml (2 cups) Guinness stout or other dark beer
- 500ml (2 cups) beef broth
- 2 tablespoons tomato paste
- 2 bay leaves
- 2 sprigs fresh thyme
- 2 tablespoons Worcestershire sauce
- 2 tablespoons brown sugar (optional)
- 2 cups diced potatoes
- Chopped fresh parsley for garnish (optional)

Instructions:

1. Season the beef pieces with salt and pepper to taste.
2. Heat the olive oil in a large pot or Dutch oven over medium-high heat. Add the beef pieces in batches and brown them on all sides. Remove the browned beef pieces from the pot and set aside.
3. In the same pot, add the chopped onions, carrots, and celery. Cook, stirring occasionally, until the vegetables are softened, about 5-7 minutes.
4. Add the minced garlic to the pot and cook for another minute, until fragrant.
5. Sprinkle the flour over the vegetables in the pot and stir to coat evenly.
6. Return the browned beef pieces to the pot. Pour in the Guinness stout and beef broth, stirring to combine.
7. Stir in the tomato paste, bay leaves, fresh thyme, Worcestershire sauce, and brown sugar (if using).
8. Bring the stew to a simmer, then reduce the heat to low. Cover the pot and let the stew simmer gently for about 1.5 to 2 hours, or until the beef is tender.

9. Once the beef is tender, stir in the diced potatoes and continue to simmer the stew for another 30 minutes, or until the potatoes are cooked through.
10. Taste the stew and adjust the seasoning with salt and pepper if needed.
11. Once done, remove the bay leaves and thyme sprigs from the stew.
12. Serve the beef and Guinness stew hot, garnished with chopped fresh parsley if desired.

Enjoy your homemade beef and Guinness stew, a comforting and satisfying dish that's perfect for sharing with family and friends!